THE SHIRLEY TEMPLE SCRAPBOOK

by Loraine Burdick

JONATHAN DAVID PUBLISHERS
MIDDLE VILLAGE, N. Y. 11379

THE SHIRLEY TEMPLE SCRAPBOOK
by
Loraine Burdick

Copyright © 1975
by
Jonathan David Publishers

No part of this book may be reproduced in any manner without written permission from the publishers. Address all inquiries to:

Jonathan David Publishers
68-22 Eliot Avenue
Middle Village, N.Y. 11379

Library of Congress Cataloging in Publication Data

Burdick, Loraine.
  The Shirley Temple scrapbook

  1. Temple, Shirley, 1928- I. Title.
PN2287.T33B8   791.43'028'0924 [B]   74-31298
ISBN 0-8246-0277-3 paperback
Paperback edition ©1982

10 9 8 7 6 5 4 3 2 1

Contents

Acknowledgments

For their kind assistance, grateful thanks are due the Shirley Temple Collectors Club and all its members, especially Nancy Schippnick, Pat Schoonmaker, Jackie Musgrave and Juanita Ciolek. Appreciation must also be expressed to Tom Fulbright (who invented Rosemaries for silent stars), Lucille McClure, Carl Hammer, Lillian Spencer, Bob Harman, Twentieth Century-Fox, Metro-Goldwyn-Mayer, Inc., and my many collector friends who shared items from all over the world. My thanks to Jack Scagnetti for his editorial assistance, and most of all, my profound thanks and appreciation to Mr. and Mrs. Charles Black.

L.B.

Foreword

Much has been written about Shirley Temple. A great deal of it has been highly exaggerated—and quite a bit untrue. This is the fate of most famous people—particularly an actress so adored by the public as was Shirley Temple. She was probably the youngest person on record to truly capture the hearts of her countrymen.

The offstage role Shirley Temple was called upon to play was much more difficult that the onstage role. It was difficult facing those pressing crowds anxious to tell her how much they loved her. And this process continued on for many years. It was one she had to contend with even as an adult.

To each person who was able to get to her after an appearance, the knowledge that they had seen her, heard her, or touched her was an unforgettable experience. But to Shirley Temple it was eternal hardship.

Shirley Temple was a beautiful and talented child. When she had reached the "ripe old" age of four, she held hands with the world. Everyone was in love with her.

Now, having reached the age of "grandmotherhood," (although she is not yet, as of this writing, a grandmother) Shirley Temple (Charles) Black is still holding hands with the world.

In this book I hope to focus in on that love affair as I have observed it over many years—ten of them in which I served as founder of the Shirley Temple Collectors and Fans Club and editor of its monthly publication. In 1970, I relinquished my role as editor, but the club is still active, and is under the guidance of Mrs. Robert Musgrave of Anchorage, Alaska.

I hope you will find as much pleasure reading and thumbing through the pages of this book as I had in preparing it.

LORAINE BURDICK

1
THE EARLY YEARS

One of the earliest, unpublished photos of Shirley as a toddler.

Little Miss Miracle

Shirley Jane Temple, who by the time she was six years old had been dubbed by the Hollywood moguls as "Little Miss Miracle," was born on April 23, 1928, at Santa Monica Hospital, Santa Monica, California. She was exactly average in weight: 6½ pounds.

It wasn't long before the depressing, fearful years of 1929 hit the Temple family as it did the rest of America. George and Gertrude Temple, the parents of Shirley Temple, had to watch their budgets carefully in order to support young Shirley and her two older brothers—John (Jack) who was 12, and George, Jr. (Sonny) who was 8.

Since the age span between baby Shirley and her brothers was so great, Gertrude had sufficient free time to devote to her cute little baby. She once admitted, "Long before she was born I tried to influence her future life by association with music, art, and natural beauty. Perhaps this prenatal preparation helped make Shirley what she is today." Undoubtedly, these goals did help shape Shirley's future.

Despite the tight family budget, the mother squeezed out enough to pay for a program that provided her baby with the best diet, exercise and vitamins and all that would assure her good health. This program protected Shirley and she was spared the childhood diseases from which most children suffer.

One interesting thing mother Gertrude did was to buy a coupon from a photographer who then took a portrait of Shirley every six months until she was two, and afterwards once a year until her sixth birthday. Some of these invaluable photographs are still extant.

Like any other mother, Mrs. Temple sang and played the radio as she did her own housework. Shirley followed her around, acting out the music that was being played. She did little fun dance steps and showed herself to be a very graceful child. Her sense of rhythm and the pleasure she derived from moving about to music was clearly in evidence at a very early age.

Shirley attempted to keep all of the puppies in the basket—but they weren't all very agreeable.

At lunch-time, games involving words and multiplication tables were played and gave Shirley a good head start. She showed all the signs of being an exceptionally capable and talented child.

When Shirley was three, Mrs. Temple decided it would be fun for Shirley to go to dancing school. Although this called for another family sacrifice, the expense of the lessons was considered worthwhile. The family enjoyed Shirley's happy stepping as much as the child.

Shirley had an inborn desire to please, and at dancing school she listened, she tried, and she loved what she was doing. She practiced the steps and learned them well, without too much effort. Shirley grew and developed, and with it came a sense of balance and symmetry. It was a beautiful thing to behold.

The school in which baby Shirley Temple was enrolled was the Meglin Dance

Studios in Los Angeles. In 1938, her enrollment card (#203) was reproduced by *Screen Guide* and shows the exact date of enrollment to be September 13, 1931. At that time, brown-eyed, blonde Shirley Jane Temple lived at 948 24th Street in Santa Monica, California.

One day, early in 1932, excitement ran high at the dancing school. A man was coming to select children for parts in a movie. Every mother had dressed her child to the hilt, hoping to impress the movie scout. Mrs. Temple, for some unknown reason, did not hear about the interviews that were to take place. No one told her about it, and she didn't see the announcement posted on the bulletin board.

Although she didn't know it at the time, Shirley was soon to become a big star. Here, Shirley is disguised as a boy so that she can do some Christmas shopping in a Los Angeles department store without being hounded by her fans.

That day Shirley came to class in her usual blue practice costume. When Mrs. Temple saw what was happening, she was embarrassed, and was about to take Shirley home. A teacher came out to the car just as she was about to drive off, and urged Mrs. Temple to let the scout see Shirley even though she was not dressed for the occasion. She agreed and Shirley joined the other children in the parade before the scout while the anxious mothers waited outside.

The movie scout said nothing, and left. But the following week another movie scout appeared, and this time Shirley hid behind the piano along with another girl. The second scout was Charles Lamont. He was a director for Educational Studios. He coaxed the two children to come out, and Shirley impressed him greatly. She was selected for a part in a movie that the studio was about to make.

The facts are not easy to sort out. In 1936, Al Hicks, a writer for *Rural Progress Magazine* insisted that 83 different people claimed to have discovered Shirley, and his impression of what happened is that Mrs. Temple had arranged for Shirley to appear at several local affairs before she was discovered at the school where she was supposed to be taught dancing.

Hicks claims that children were beating each other with boots, and that the teacher was wild-eyed. He reported that Shirley's first day on the set was a super dud. The second day, she arrived accompanied by mother, father and doctor. The doctor stated that Shirley had had an abscessed ear, and that he had lanced it the night before. Hicks then tells how Shirley spent the day rehearsing over and over "all through that day's filming and the bellowing of a wild-eyed director." Hicks' task was to get Shirley and others signed to contracts with Jack Hays Productions, but the accuracy of the facts in the magazine article is questionable.

Mrs. George Temple, Shirley's mother and constant chaperone, reads Shirley a bedtime story.

Jack Hays had a different version of what happened during the period of Shirley's film debut. In the July, 1935 issue of *Movie Mirror*, he claimed that a woman casting-assistant located Shirley sitting stiffly upright in the waiting room and that she chose her; although actually, Audrey Rae Leonard had finally been chosen that day as the lead.

Audrey was beautiful, and had studied dramatics for a year and a half, but she lacked the appeal of little Shirley. So Audrey was scrapped. However, when Shirley failed to appear for the first day's shooting due to an ear operation, Audrey was rushed back to take over.

Whatever actually did happen, the fact has been established that Shirley received for her first day of work a paycheck totaling $10.00. This covered work for one day including overtime, for the Baby Stars Series. The check was signed by Jack Hays and dated January 9, 1932.

Shirley continued to receive $10.00 a day for working on one-reel comedies in which Educational Films Corporation, a subsidiary of Educational Pictures, Inc., was spoofing first-run features. The comedies each took about four days to make. Hays obtained 75% of his financial backing from Universal Studios to produce the first of these "baby burlesk" films. He raised the other 25% mostly from advertising products that were featured in the film. Shirley was to star in eight of these baby burlesk comedies.

The original plan called for dubbing in adult voices, but with the pilot film, *The Runt Page*, it was discovered that the children's voices sounded much more comic and, as a result, so much more acceptable to the public. The children did not have to be real-life diaper tots, but there was a height limit of 36 inches established as the norm.

The first filmed and exhibited "baby burlesk" movie was *War Babies*. It was a take-off on the World War I film *What Price Glory?* In *War Babies*, Shirley imitated Dolores Del Rio, playing the part of Charmaine. She spoke most of her lines in French, including what are quoted as her first screen words, *Mais oui, mon cher*. She had her own little soldier boys to vamp, and girlish competition which she overcame by a toss of her bare shoulder and a kiss.

She had other interesting roles in the "baby burlesk" series. She impersonated Louella Parsons as Lulu Parsnips and played Marlene Dietrich as Moreles Sweetrick.

She played a missionary called Diaperzan in which Danny Boone, Jr. played Tarzan in *Kid in Africa*.

In *Glad Rags to Riches*, she played La Belle Diaper, a show girl, and sang her first song, "She's Only a Bird in a Gilded Cage."

In *The Kid's Last Stand*, a burlesk of the great Jack Dempsey, and the world of boxing, thugs kidnapped Shirley to influence the championship bout.

In *Polly-Tix in Washington*, a burlesk of the capital's political scene, Shirley was dressed in two-piece black lace undies for a provocative look of a political golddigger.

In *The Pie-Covered Wagon*, a spoof of the big film, *The Covered Wagon*, she was tied to a stake while "Indians" pelted her with dirt.

When the kiddie capers waned, Shirley was cast in another series, *Frolics of Youth*, and during this time, Jack Hays had an option on her future work. He used her to promote his own school designed to create child movie stars. Many eager parents were happy to send their children and pay the tuition fee.

The Meglin Kiddies School, based in Los Angeles, built up to a clientele of 10,000 children across the country in 40 Meglin schools. They offered classes in dancing, drama, singing and gymnastics especially for amateurs, but also for professionals who paid a higher fee. Other schools, both legitimate and otherwise, imitated Meglin. The schools, for the most part, gave eager kids and pushy mothers a bit of training which would come in handy whenever they mobbed studios to answer casting advertisements.

Hays either felt that the schools were more profitable to him than any actual studio work, or else he simply lacked studio contacts to go any further with Shirley's film career. Eventually, the Educational Studios filed for bankruptcy. However, Mr. Temple had bought out Shirley's contract long before that. Still, this didn't prevent two later lawsuits by Hays when Shirley became a star. In 1936, he asked for a million dollars, claiming credit for training Shirley for stardom. In 1939, he filed again, this time seeking $700,000. He lost both suits.

Before Hays instituted his suits, Elinor O'Reilly and Gene Mann sued the Temples claiming they had a five-year contract with them, and had lined up engagements for Shirley, including four weeks of personal appearances in New York at $7,500.00 per week. This case was settled out of court, and it is not known whether there was any truth to these suits or whether it was simply a case of people wanting to cash in on the Temple gold mine. Mr. and Mrs. Temple had to stave off countless opportunists, such as approaches from unscrupulous life insurance agents, individuals and organizations seeking donations, endorsements, and attempts of all kinds to help themselves at the expense of the Temple family.

It is difficult to trace accurately many of the early acting parts of Shirley's career. On her own, Mrs. Temple evidently visited many casting offices, hunting for bit parts for Shirley, aside from the opportunities that came from Educational's operation. Mrs. Temple spent countless hours trying to find the right parts and the right places for Shirley to work. She landed a small part in *To the Last Man*, a Paramount western released late in 1933. Harpo Marx, who was making a film at Paramount at the same time, allegedly offered Mrs. Temple $50,000 to adopt Shirley, but he was, of course, turned down.

Paramount let Shirley go after the western, and Fox Film Corporation didn't keep her either after she did a part in *Carolina* with Janet Gaynor, Lionel Barrymore and Robert Young.

A short time later, in December, 1933, Leo Houck, assistant director for Fox Film Corporation, and Jay Gorney, a song writer, asked Mrs. Temple if Shirley could sing. The studio had already been interviewing children for their upcoming musical, and schedule pressures were mounting. As yet, they had not found anyone who was suitable for the part. Shirley auditioned for Lew Brown, associate producer of a picture titled, *Fox Follies*. Somebody played St. Louis Blues on the piano and Shirley did a buck-and-wing. Then, she sang a song that she had heard Rudy Vallee sing on the radio a few days earlier.

Houck broke into a smile. He was delighted. His search had ended. Gorney and

Mrs. Temple were ecstatic. Each had found what they were seeking: one, a new talent —perhaps even a star—someone who might be the right person to "make" his songs; and the other, a mother who had found others who appreciated her precious child.

Mrs. Temple exuded excitement and pride over Shirley's first full-length film starring role. she was a proud mother eager to share her darling child with others, and to bring them a measure of happiness. Later, she explained her inner-feelings as she saw so many people reaching out, patting, and admiring her adorable offspring. To Mrs. Temple, it was her contribution to a depressed world trapped and wallowing in the quicksand of the miseries of the early years of the 1930s.

The Hays Office, which censored films, was anxious to clean up the movies, and Shirley had come along at the right time.

Fox changed the name of Shirley's first starring film, released in 1934, to *Stand Up and Cheer*, starring Warner Baxter and James Dunn. Seeing and hearing Shirley, audiences and critics did exactly that: they stood up and screamed with delight. She had captured the nation's heart. She was lovable and adorable in her several scenes of follies production numbers.

Fox responded, too. The studio negotiated a seven-year contract for her increasing her salary from $75.00 to $150.00 per week. When the happy news of record attendance in New York City theaters reached Hollywood, Fox moved Shirley's name

When Shirley received a special Oscar in 1935 from famous writer Irvin S. Cobb, every wire service and hundreds of photographers covered the event.

higher up on the theater marquee and began plans for her to make another film.

And so began the ascent of a sparkling star who started an acting career at the age of four, became a star at six, and between 1935 and 1938 won an Oscar and was the number one box office attraction.

She performed like a doll on the screen, and was copied by the Ideal Toy Corporation to be a doll-friend for girls. Dubbed versions of her pictures played throughout the world, and foreign newspapers carried her photographs almost like front page news. She had become the world's darling before she finished elementary school.

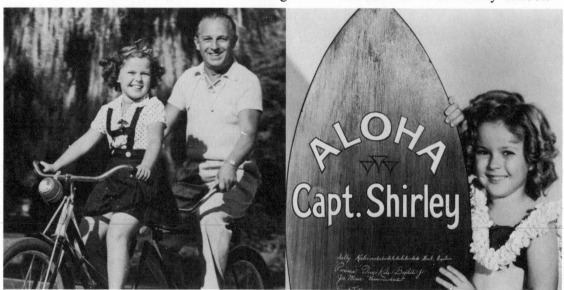

(Left) Shirley Temple, who had recently celebrated her ninth birthday, joined her father on this bicycle built for two. They were happily pedaling along the paths of Palm Springs, California, when this candid shot was taken. (Right) The Twentieth Century-Fox star was presented with this unique surfboard by her Hawaiian friends when she visited Honolulu for a brief vacation in 1935.

Meanwhile, Paramount executives were beginning to pay attention to reports from people who had been involved with Shirley in *To the Last Man*, the western in which she had a small part. Paramount was hunting for a little girl and, from what they heard, here might be the answer to a problem that had been gnawing away at them.

The studio had been holding the story, *Little Miss Marker*, for two years, unable to find a child star. They scrutinized Shirley carefully, and decided that she was just right for the part. Paramount negotiated with Fox to loan Shirley at $1,000 a week. The deal was arranged and she appeared with Adolph Menjou.

With the release, in June, 1934, of Paramount's *Little Miss Marker*, Fox was convinced that they had a star on their hands. When it was suggested to Mr. and Mrs. Temple that they break the Fox contract, and take Shirley elsewhere for more money, the Temples thought it proper to persuade Fox to give Shirley a substantial raise. They requested $2,500 a week. Fox countered with an offer of $1,000.

In late July, 1934, about three months after *Stand Up and Cheer* had been released, a new contract was signed with Fox for $1,250 a week. Increases were built in that would extend over the next seven years.

This was a great deal of money to be earned in the 1930s, but Fox was amply rewarded, for in fulfilling her contract to make three pictures per year, the studio grossed about six million dollars a year from the little girls' talents.

About $300.00 per picture was funneled into the Shirley Temple Milk Fund, which built up equity from actors and crew members fined for assorted misdemeanors. It also earned a "salary" for the acting of Shirley's dogs and horses.

Shirley's third Fox contract specified that she receive no praise from co-workers, except from her mother and her director, and also that she be prohibited from viewing films of other actors lest she copy mannerisms and be influenced by them. The studio feared that this might possibly result in altering her distinctive, natural style and in changing her lovely personality.

Mrs. Temple received a salary of $150.00 a week for the care and coaching of Shirley, as well as for being her sole hairdresser. Shirley was now given her very own bungalow on the Fox lot.

No American company would assume the liability of insuring Shirley against an accident, so a British firm was found, which covered her with a $25,000 policy. The policy specified that she should not fly in an airplane or go into a war area. By 1935, Shirley Temple and Will Rogers were the most valuable properties at Fox.

Mrs. Temple was an essential ingredient in the successful career of her daughter. All of her time was devoted to Shirley and this meant many personal sacrifices. Her life was not her own.

Although she hired a housekeeper, and engaged a cook, each day had to be planned with Shirley's schedule in mind. She made a stoic effort to see to it that the family's attention not be totally focused on Shirley, but that was a practically impossible objective.

Each evening had to include the learning of lines for the next day's work if a new scene was to be shot. Several read-throughs would precede Shirley's rapid recital of the lines until she had the script down pat. Then Mrs. Temple slowed her down to deliver each phrase with proper speed, gesture and emphasis. By morning Shirley still knew her lines perfectly—along with everyone else's who was in the scene.

Shirley's increased earnings enabled the Temples to move into a larger house, in Santa Monica, and send George Jr. to military school. The new house had ample space for a fan mail office plus two secluded play areas for Shirley. The new house offered more privacy from overly eager fans who, in the past, would peer through windows and knock at the door at all hours.

The Temples used some of Shirley's earnings to pay for sundry expenses, including clothing. Some of these items included a glass-brick playhouse, care and housing for her animals, and other play features that were necessary when she could no longer go to the beach without being mobbed, or visit a store lest people crowd and jostle her. Before this, one woman did not hesitate to take out a pair of scissors in the middle of a crowded store, and snip off one of Shirley's curls.

Luncheons at the Fox commissary were stopped because Shirley ate so slowly, and so many stars and members of the studio staff would stop to visit with her and to admire her. This was distracting and interfered with Shirley's performances. The Fox contract specified that Shirley would work only as long as it didn't harm her personal life and happiness. That harm included becoming overly self-confident or an egotistical showoff. Mrs. Temple worked very hard to circumvent this for the good of her daughter, and Fox cooperated for the good of its gold mine.

After the filming of *The Littlest Rebel*, in 1935, Fox provided Shirley with a portable dressing room. This gave her added quiet and much-needed seclusion from an over-attentive adult world.

Work at the studio, nevertheless, had its days of fun for Shirley, and interesting things were always happening. A teacher was always on hand to instruct Shirley and particularly to make sure that the proper hours of schooling and work, as set by law, were fulfilled. Adult movie stars and members of the film crew did all they could to make her waits between scenes interesting.

During the film *Now and Forever*, in 1934, actor Gary Cooper taught her to draw, and bought her a teddy bear named Grumpy. During the same film, actress Dorothy Dell was killed in an auto accident. Mournful cast members tried to keep the news from Shirley, but she heard about it and she sobbed in Carole Lombard's arms.

Will Rogers was a close friend of Shirley's and she had hoped to be able to make a movie with him. While on a vacation in Hawaii, she learned of the death of Will Rogers in a crash of a private plane piloted by Wiley Post in Alaska, in 1935. Her wish

Will Rogers poses for a picture with Shirley Temple not long after she was awarded a long-term contract with Fox.

was never fulfilled, but she did have the honor of participating that fall in the dedication of the new sound stage at Fox in memory of Rogers. When she unveiled the plaque in his memory, her simple statement brought handkerchiefs to the eyes of every person in attendance. "I loved him, too," she said tearfully.

During the filming of *Captain January*, in which she starred with Guy Kibbee, the new Fox sound stage was put into use for the first time. Fox technicians constructed an 80-foot square pool which was to serve as a port. It was four feet deep and had a capacity of 143,616 gallons of water. The stage accommodated two full-rigged fishing boats plus a coast-guard cutter, requiring workmen on three sides to operate agitators for wave-making. Vaporized mineral oil was cooled over dry ice to make a low-hanging fog over the water.

Although Shirley had made the boat trip to Hawaii without getting seasick, she did become seasick on the Fox pond, and shooting was delayed. In this film, she performed a difficult dance sequence on circular stairs.

During her years as a child star, the publicity releases proclaimed that Shirley was a child prodigy and genius. Psychologists who tested her to determine her mental capacity concluded that she was indeed bright, but not a prodigy. In January, 1936, *Screen Play* magazine published her IQ as 155, 55 points above the average.

Shirley's ears were as sharp as her mind. When a columnist visited her bungalow and interviewed Mrs. Temple asking about Shirley's preferences and about her diet, Shirley played quietly for awhile, as though totally unaware. Then, suddenly, she asked: "Why don't you interview me? I'm the star."

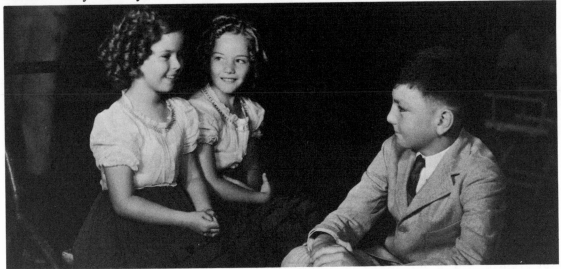

A public relations shot taken in 1937 shows Shirley and her look-alike stand-in, Mary Lou Isleib, being interviewed.

Shirley loved to have her own games on the set. Sometimes the assistant director, Booh McCracken, would call her to a scene and then have to circle her dressing room, count to 10, or be tied by her to a chair before work could progress. She would go exploring about the set or beyond, and hide in small out-of-the way places. She would not always come out when called.

Director Harry Lachman, aware of her prompt responses to lines and cues, brought a duck call to the set and announced that it was her own private cue call. No one was to answer to that call but she, and when he blew it, that meant that she must come. This device solved the problem. It was a lot easier than hunting for her when she preferred to play the game of hide 'n seek. When Shirley's mother was on the set, the new-fangled device was not always necessary. Whatever the problem or game, a glance at Mrs. Temple was usually enough to establish calm and get things down to business. Mrs. Temple was a strict and respected disciplinarian. With her around, Shirley took her work and play seriously, and most of the time enjoyed both.

Shirley was carefully protected on the set from being exposed to obscene words. On the *Captain January* set, a parrot was sent back to its trainer because it had a vocabulary which was quite indelicate. Fortunately, it was discovered before Shirley had arrived on the scene, and the problem was avoided.

Shirley's vocabulary in *The Littlest Rebel* did include the use of "damn" along with "Yankee," but her words were always carefully chosen because they were imitated by children all over the world. Writers praised her vocabulary which was reported to be 750 words while the average adult only had a vocabulary of about 450 words. Probably, a more realistic explanation of this extensive vocabulary is that it contained many words which were studio slang and movie lingo—not in popular use.

During Shirley's filming of *The Littlest Rebel*, in 1935 at age 7, Buddy DeSylva came up with the great idea for a scene in which Shirley would plead with President Lincoln for the lives of her father and the Yankee Colonel. Shirley, overhearing the idea, announced: "Of course the pardon has to be granted. We can't make a heavy out of Lincoln."

Writer Vincent Mahoney said of Shirley: "She shows a certain impish sophistication, but it can just as easily be diagnosed as the natural fiendishness of an intelligent and healthy child."

Shirley's diet was of much more concern than her vocabulary and intelligence. Her weekly menu, prepared by baby specialist, Dr. Russell Sands, included spinach on four of the seven days. Those were the days of "Popeye" when kids hated spinach, but parents believed the nutritionists who said spinach contains iron, and iron is good for the body. One day Shirley hatched a plot with the commissary staff to have her mother served a whole plateful of tasteless spinach instead of the lunch she ordered. In the film, *Poor Little Rich Girl*, she even had a song urging, "You Gotta Eat Your Spinach, Baby."

Shirley Temple quickly became a legend, and as is the case with most legends, it is sometimes difficult to separate fact from fiction. Mrs. Temple wrote in a 1934 article that Shirley was taught to be confident and self-reliant so she would not be afraid—not even to rearing horses, as she did in *Little Miss Marker*. However, another account told of Mrs. Temple working for three days to persuade Shirley to tap dance on the piano, and then fling herself into John Boles' arms in the film *Curly Top*.

The 1930s was an era when such traits as beauty, neatness, honesty and religiosity were admired, so naturally her publicity emphasized how generously Shirley was endowed in all of these areas. And the whole world accepted and was influenced by what they saw in her and read about her. Patricia Hill, writing for a British fan magazine, commented: "It is no exaggeration to say that Shirley's charm has done as much to lift the world out of its depression, by lightening the hearts of all who see her, as any of the wordy conferences that have been held by statesmen all over the world.

A fantastic number of Shirley Temple dolls were produced over the years, and Shirley did her share of promotional work.

Her film *Bright Eyes*, in 1934, broke all Christmas day records at the Paramount in Portland, Oregon. The box-office took in $2,500. *Curly Top* was a smash hit at the fabulous New York City Music Hall, which seated more than 5,000 people at one showing. Several times during the day, the management had to stop selling tickets, because the long lines waiting to get in were greater than the theater's seating capacity.

Shirley Temple was making fantastic amounts of money for her film studio and for theaters throughout the country. She was helping the nation, too, for a large portion of her half-million-odd dollars a year in salary and endorsements had to be paid out in the form of federal and state income taxes. One estimate is that her net take was perhaps $100,000 per year. Ironically, but understandably, her mother gave her a personal allowance which was reported at four dollars and twenty-five cents.

Shirley exhibits a few of the dolls showered upon her by fans during her two-week stay in Hawaii prior to filming *The Littlest Rebel*.

The sale of Shirley Temple dolls probably saved the Ideal Toy Company from bankruptcy. The 1930s were the years of the great depression, and Shirley's film success was undoubtedly responsible for many people finding employment in some venture for which she was directly or indirectly responsible.

Irvin Cobb, in presenting Shirley with a special Oscar on February 27, 1935, said:

> Darling, when Santa Claus bundled you up, a fragrant, delicious, dimpling, joyous, doll-baby package, and dropped you down Creation's chimney, he gave to mankind the dearest and the sweetest Christmas present that ever gladdened the hearts and stirred the souls of this weary old world . . . Through your instinctive art and your natural artistry, millions upon millions of children have been made to laugh, and millions of older folks have laughed with them.

On March 14, 1935, at the premiere of *The Little Colonel*, Shirley expressed her feelings towards the world when she "signed" the cement near her footprint, at Grauman's Chinese Theatre in Hollywood, large block letters:

LOVE TO YOU ALL —SHIRLEY TEMPLE

She usually signed autographs with that same expression of love. She once explained it to a questioner, "I can't sign them 'Your friend,' because I don't even know them. But since I love everybody, it is telling the truth to sign them 'Love, Shirley Temple.' "

By 1935, Shirley Temple's popularity had reached such proportions that her fan mail was about 5,000 letters per week. They were delivered daily by truck. One room of the Santa Monica home was set aside for her fan mail and secretary.

Most letters were answered the same day. Frequently, a postcard was sent explaining that upon receipt of a dime (which really didn't cover the cost) a photograph would be mailed.

After filming *The Little Colonel*, Shirley was honored by The American Legion.
She was given a certificate and a medal indicating that she was a "real" colonel.

Shirley posed for an average of 20 photographs a day just to cover fan and publicity requests. This usually took about an hour, but she was patient and endured the grind bravely. At one point as many as 10 secretaries were employed at the Fox studios to handle her mail because about 10,000 letters per week were pouring in.

Because the Temples had signed up for a portrait album and sittings every six months, professional baby pictures were available for inclusion with later publicity showing her as a chubby tot. Even going back to her days at Paramount, publicity men for studios posed her with various famous people, and later nearly all celebrities sought the privilege of posing with Shirley.

She posed for various national, social, civic and community groups to publicize national holidays and to advertise her movies and promote articles bearing her name. Shirley Temple reached out into nearly every area of life, and her presence was felt in nearly every country throughout the world through the moving films that made her name and face unforgettable. Whatever she did or wore or endorsed was coveted.

Clothes were patterned after hers, whether homemade or store-bought. Shirley didn't like ruffles at the neck or fussy clothes, which made her a good model for children's wear. She protested wearing a towel about her neck as many adult stars did to protect their costumes from being soiled by makeup between film takes. After much work in cleaning makeup off her clothes, wardrobe lady Hulda Anderson came up with the idea of Shirley wearing extra collars between takes to protect the clothes from the makeup.

As a youngster, Shirley Temple was probably the most photographed person in the world. Here she is with a Twentieth Century-Fox photographer, Anthony Ugrin, who took more than 7,500 photographs of her over a two year period.

Besides actual costumes worn in movies, Shirley Temple fashions were sold in ready-to-wear department stores. From the start, Mrs. Temple emphasized quality in the construction of anything that bore her daughter's name and likeness. With the dresses, she insisted that Shirley had to have actually worn the dress before it could be promoted. This meant sessions with Shirley trying on a great many dresses, and posing in them. The dresses and other Shirley Temple-endorsed garments were by style, price and construction in the higher price range. Because of the poor economic situation in the 1930s, many little girls had to be happy with only one Shirley Temple dress. (They would rather have one Shirley Temple dress than two or three dresses of the average type in the average price range.) The dresses were especially treasured by youngsters and were saved for special occasions and as souvenirs.

There were also many varieties of Shirley Temple accessories which appeared on the market. These included soap novelties in a variety of forms including cameo portraits and figurines.

Assorted tablewear items were tied in with Shirley Temple, such as dishes, cereal bowls, drinking mugs.

Paper doll look-alikes of Shirley Temple were among the most treasured playthings for girls. Saalfield's first book of paper dolls of Shirley Temple in 1934 sold over six million copies and was later reissued (in a thinner cover). There has been talk of reissuing these paper dolls. Saalfield also published a line of paper cover picture booklets on Shirley's childhood star days, illustrating stories of her films, and coloring books.

Shirley presents Walt Disney with his Oscar for the award-winning 1938 production, *Snow White and the Seven Dwarfs*.

Stationery, school notebooks, and slates, and greeting cards used Shirley Temple designs.

Sam Fox Publishing Company released sheet music and song albums on Shirley Temple.

Magazines, newspapers and theaters organized Shirley Temple clubs for promotional purposes, and all provided fun for the kiddies. They also conducted

Shirley Temple contests, including look-alike contests. Beauty shops did big business imitating Shirley's hair style.

A non-alcoholic fruit drink was named "The Shirley Temple."

Many children, inspired by the Shirley Temple image, tried to imitate her. They took tap dancing lessons, singing lessons, and drama lessons, and entered talent contests. Even children with ordinary looks and no talent were urged by pushy mothers to try and become a Shirley Temple; hopeful that fame and riches might come their way.

Many fans sent gifts to Shirley, particularly at Christmastime. Various publicity projects also were a source of gifts. She was unable to keep a kangaroo from Australia because it kept jumping the fence and running off. A Shetland pony given to her by Joseph Schenck came from Britain accompanied by a caretaker. It became part of her private menage, even appearing in a film with her. A cow, Tilly of Tillamook, Oregon,

This little calf was named Tillie Temple, and was sent to Shirley as a gift from 500 children from Tillamook, Oregon as a token of appreciation for her outstanding work in motion pictures.

On a cross-country trip in 1938, Shirley visited with G-Man J. Edgar Hoover. Hoover arranged for her father to do some shooting on the FBI's firing range, and Shirley paid for it with a big kiss.

grew from a gift calf, and had to be boarded at a dairy. Many gifts had to be returned, while others were turned over to various charities. By 1936, some fans were writing to her and asking for gifts of dolls instead of photos.

On Shirley's eighth birthday, Fox held a party at its Cafe de Paris with 150 guests. Shirley begged for no photos to interrupt the fun. She received over 1,000 birthday cakes from fans, including one from the Governor of Tennessee—a gigantic one, shaped like that state's capitol.

As the years and the films wore on, reviewers became more critical of her films' stories, while still praising Shirley's talents. They felt that it was wrong for her to be the whole show, and that the plot should be more than just a showcase for her talents. Still, Fox liked her as she was—a song and dance girl who could pout and turn on a stream of tears when called for.

Finally, Mrs. Temple gave vent to her own strong feelings about Shirley's stories, something in which she had not previously interfered. One report was that Darryl Zanuck, head of Fox studios, pushed Shirley into the more dramatic pictures while the Temples favored continuing singing and dancing. Mrs. Temple rated *Just Around the Corner*, released in 1938, as a bad story. So did many reviewers. She rated *The Little Princess*, a 1939 release, much higher in story and production quality, and said Shirley's popularity, which had been dropping, rose as the result of it.

A 1940 release, *Young People*, was not the hit anticipated. When the Temples learned that it was to be followed by a two-year-old scenario which revolved about all Shirley's old song and dance tricks, the parents suddenly took action. They felt that with the war in Europe sealing off Fox's overseas markets, it would be a good time for a change. Rather than reduce Shirley to making low-budget near-B pictures, they were willing to give up her $5,000 per week salary, Mrs. Temple's $750 per week and Mr. Temple's occasional fee as an actor's agent. So the Fox contract was terminated in 1940 by mutual consent.

Mrs. Temple wanted a more natural life for Shirley—fewer pictures, regular public schooling, and friends apart from the studio. Shirley entered the private Westlake School for Girls in the seventh grade.

1932 FILMS

The Runt Page Educational Films Corp., subsidiary of Educational Pictures, Inc. 1932.
This 10-minute film was a spoof on the dramatic film, *The Front Page*, a story about newspaper people. All the characters were pre-school children.

Shirley Temple ....Lulu Parsnips (Louella Parsons)
Georgie Smith.......................Raymond Bunion (Damon Runyon)
Unknown ....Bears Bugs (Arthur ''Bugs'' Baer)
Directed by Roy LaVerne
Produced by Jack Hays

War Babies Educational Films Corp. 1932.
This short film was a spoof on the big, dramatic war film, *What Price Glory?* The plot revolved around soldiers coming to the milk bar to meet girls.

Shirley Temple ....Charmaine, French girl
Georgie Smith..Soldier boyfriend
Eugene Butler ....Soldier boyfriend
Directed by Charles Lamont
Produced by Jack Hays

The Pie-Covered Wagon Educational Films Corp. 1932.
A spoof of the major film, *The Covered Wagon*, the plot called for the Indians to raid a little wagon train. Shirley Temple plays the role of one of the main captives who was later rescued.

Shirley Temple
Georgie Smith
Cowboys and Indians
Directed by Charles Lamont
Produced and written by Jack Hays
Photographed by Dwight Warren

Glad Rags to Riches Educational Films Corp. 1932.
A poor but pretty girl goes from rags to riches in show business. Shirley sang her first film song, ''She's Only a Bird in a Gilded Cage.''

Shirley Temple ....La Belle Diaper, showgirl
Eugene Butler ....her escort
Marilyn Granas (later Shirley's first stand-in)
Georgie Smith

The Kid's Last Stand Educational Films Corp. 1932.
Thugs kidnap the boxer's girl, attempting to force him to throw the championship fight. His girl, played by Shirley, is rescued just in time for the champ to win the bout.

Shirley Temple .... Girlfriend
Georgie Smith... Diaper Dampsy, boxer
Sidney Kilbrick ....Thug

Polly-Tix in Washington Educational Films Corp. 1932.

This spoof on the Washington political scene saw Shirley in the role of an influential and wealthy woman helping to elect a politician to office.

Shirley Temple ....Political gold-digger
Georgie Smith.. Cowboy politician
Gloria Ann Mack

Kiddin' Hollywood Educational Films Corp. 1932.

A temperamental film star who wouldn't do her job is replaced by a floor-scrubbing girl and she becomes the new star. Shirley's character was a spoof on Marlene Dietrich.

Shirley Temple .... Morelegs Sweetrick
Georgie Smith................................. Frightwig Von Stumblebum

Kiddin' Africa Educational Films Corp. 1932.

A missionary, in Africa to civilize cannibals, is captured and later rescued by "Tarzan," who she marries and domesticates.

Shirley Temple ....Madame Cradlebait who later became
Mrs. Diaperzan
Danny Boone, Jr..Diaperzan
Cannibals
A preacher man

Some of the financial backing for burlesk productions like *War Babies* was secured by advertising products such as Kellogg's Corn Flakes.

In the 1932 film, *War Babies*, a milk bar was the hang-out for doughboys Georgie Smith and Eugene Butler. Shirley seems quite natural playing the part of a flirt.

A rare, pensive shot of Shirley taken from the burlesk movie, *A Pie-Covered Wagon*.

Eugene Butler and Georgie Smith join Shirley in this cowboy and Indian scene from *The Pie-Covered Wagon*. Georgie took a lot of punishment, and Shirley looks on in amazement.

This sober portrait shows the child star in a scene from *Glad Rags to Riches*.

Director Charles Lamont is showing Shirley just where to fix her eyes in order to get the proper sultry pose. She burlesks Marlene Dietrich in the 1932 film, *Kiddin' Hollywood*.

FRIGHTWIG VON STUMBLEBUM

"The Mad Genius"

The scene is at Grauman's Chinese Theatre, just above the footprints of Doug Fairbanks. A touch of realism is added to *Kiddin' Hollywood* with this spoof on Von Stroheim. Georgie Smith is standing alongside the poster.

In *Polly-Tix in Washington*, Shirley takes her campaign very seriously. Here, in her boudoir, she plans political strategy, while her maid, Marilyn Granas, waits on her.

Everyone was on the bandwagon during the political campaign of cowboy Georgie Smith. Shirley and Gloria Ann White support his candidacy in the 1933 film, *Polly-Tix in Washington*.

In the film, *Kiddin' Africa*, Shirley visits with Danny Boone, Jr. He is dressed as Tarzan while she sits comfortably on a towel.

The opening scene in *Kiddin' Africa* finds Shirley portraying the role of a missionary in the wilds of Africa. Her servants in this scene later double as cannibals.

1933 FILMS

The Red-Haired Alibi Tower Productions, Inc. 1933.
A man in trouble with the law has a girlfriend who is his alibi when she becomes interested in his little girl, played by Shirley.

Myrna Kennedy ....Lynn Monith
Theo. Von Eltz .... Trent Travers
Grant Withers ....Bob Shelton
Parnell Pratt .... Regan
Huntley Gordon ....Kente
Fred Kelsey ....Corcoran
John Vosburgh ....Morgan
Marion Lessing ....Bee Lee
Shirley Temple .... Gloria
Paul Porcasi .... Margoli
Arthur Hoyt ....Henri
Story by Wilson Collison
Directed by Christy Cabanne
Screenplay by Edward T. Lowe

Merrily Yours Educational Films Corp. 1933.
This comedy saw Shirley as a little sister who disrupts her brother's household chores. He hurriedly seeks to finish so he can go to a dance and meet a new girl.

Junior Coughlin or Coghlan ....Sonny Rogers
Kenneth Howell ....Harry Vanderpool
Mary Blackford ....Phyllis Dean
Shirley Temple ....Mary Lou Rogers
Sidney Miller .... Harry's "stooge"
Harry Myers... Mr. Rogers
Helene Chadwick ....Mrs. Rogers
Lloyd Ingraham .... Mr. Dean
Thelma Hill..Betty
Isabel La Mal ....Mrs. Vanderpool
Directed and written by Charles Lamont
Photographed by Dwight Warren
Western Electric Noiseless Recording

Out All Night Universal. 1933.
Slim Summerville is forced to take his mother along on his honeymoon. Comedy sequences show him gradually cutting the apron strings.

Slim Summerville...Ronald Colgate
ZaSu Pitts ....Bonny
Laura Hope Crews ....Mrs. Colgate
Shirley Grey..Kate
Alexander Carr...Rosemountain
Rollo Lloyd .... Arnold
Billy Barty, Shirley Temple, Phillip Purdy ....Children
Gene Lewis... Tracy
Also: Florence Enright, Dorothy Bay, Mae Busch, Paul Hurst
Story by Tim Whelan
Screenplay by William Anthony McGuire
Directed by Sam Taylor

In *Merrily Yours*, Isabel LaMal reprimands Junior Coghlan for doing a very bad job of tending the lawn, but it was really Shirley's fault.

Dora's Dunking Doughnuts Educational Films Corp. 1933.
A doughnut shop, going into deep financial trouble, is saved by a girl who invents a special dunking doughnut. Her fiance, a teacher, volunteers his music class to promote the doughnut on radio.

Florence Gill ....The Barnyard Nightingale
Fern Emmett ....Mrs. Zilch
Blanche Payson ....Mrs. Blotts
Georgia O'Dell...Mrs. Ipswick
The Meglin Kids Band
Directed by Harry J. Edwards
Story and dialogue by Ernest Pagano and Ewart Adamson
Musical numbers by Alfonse Corelli

Pardon My Pups Educational Films Corp. 1933.
This short, family comedy was adapted from a full-length story, "Mild Oats."

Frank (Junior) Coughlin
Shirley Temple
Kenneth Howell
Dorothy Ward
Harry Myers
Virginia True Boardman
"Queenie" the Spaniel
Directed by Charles Lamont
Suggested by the story "Mild Oats" by Florence Ryerson and Colin Clements, adapted by Ewart Adamson

Music teacher, Andy Clyde, gives Shirley some very special attention as he tries to teach her a song in the 1933 film, *Dora's Dunking Doughnuts.*

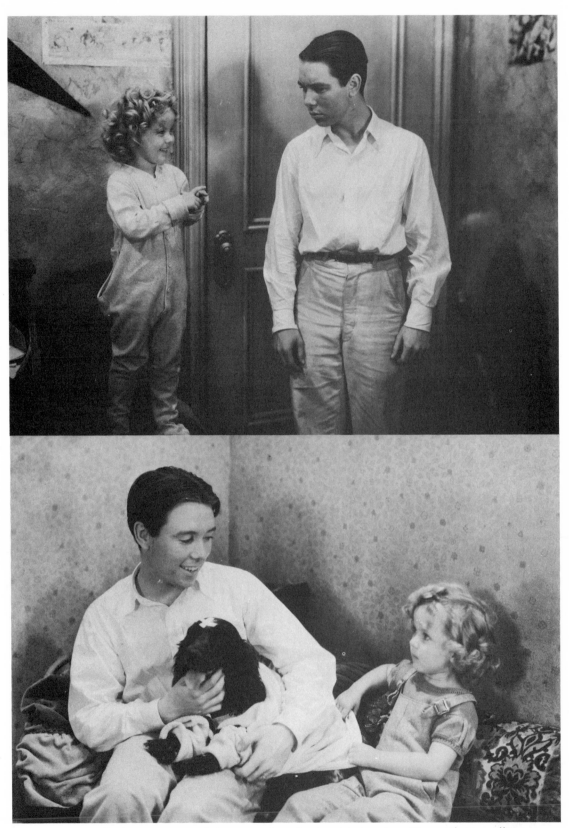

(Top) Shirley's gesture of shame is aimed at her big brother (Kenneth Howell) in *Pardon My Pups*. The drop-seated sleepers worn in the 1933 film have long gone out of style. (Bottom) Kenneth Howell and Shirley befriend the spaniel, Queenie, in another scene from *Pardon My Pups*, and patiently bandage her wounded head.

Managed Money Educational Films Corp. 1933.
   Two pals, who lack money to attend military school, go prospecting in the desert.
They meet the school's owner in the desert and he rewards them with enrollment in
the school.

   Shirley Temple .... Mary Lou
   Frank (Junior) Coughlin
   Harry Myers
   Huntly Gordon
   Directed by Charles Lamont

What To Do? Educational Films Corp. 1933.
   Just when a boy and his team were going to win the school championship, his father
announces a sudden move to another town. The son fakes illness to delay the move.

   Frank (Junior) Coughlin
   Harry Myers
   Shirley Temple
   Kenneth Howell
   Lila Leslie
   Dorothy Ward (discovered for this by Phyllis Haver)
   Broderick O'Farrell

The above scene from *Managed Money* takes place at Hollywood's Black-Fox
Military Institute, a school which has long passed into oblivion.

An unusually beautiful pose with Shirley holding a fur purse that was used in *Managed Money*, part of the Frolics of Youth series.

To the Last Man Paramount. December, 1933.

A Zane Grey western, the story is about a range war between two families, with two children growing up to love each other in spite of the feud. In the end, they secure a truce.

Randolph Scott .... Lynn Hayden
Esther Ralston ....Ellen Colby
Shirley Temple .... Mary Standing
Buster Crabbe ....Bill Hayden
Noah Beery ....Jed Colby
Jack LaRue..Jim Daggs
Barton MacLane .... Neil Standing
Gail Patrick .... Ann Hayden Standing (Shirley's mother)
Egon Brecher ....Mark Hayden
Fuzzy Knight ....Jeff Morley
James Engles ....Ely Bruce
Murial Kirkland ....Molly Hayden
Eugenie Besserer .... Granny Spelvin
Harlan Knight ....Grandpa Spelvin
John Peter Richmond..Pete Garon
Harry Cording .... Harry Malone
Erville Alderson ....Judge
James Burke...Sheriff
Jay Ward .... Lynn Hayden
Rosita Butler .... Ann Hayden
Cullen Johnson ....Bill Hayden
Russell Powell ....Greaves
Delmar Watson ....Tad Standing

All of the stars at Fox Film Studios were eager to be photographed with the five-year-old sensation. Here, Spencer Tracy takes advantage of an opportunity to pose with Shirley to help promote his new film, *Marie Galante*.

1934 FILMS

Carolina Fox Film Corp. February, 1934.
The downfall of an old Southern aristocrat family is dramatized in the clash between Yankee and rebel generals.

Janet Gaynor .... Joanna
Lionel Barrymore ....Bob Connelly
Robert Young ....Will Connelly
Henrietta Crosman ....Mrs. Connelly
Richard Cromwell.. Allen
Mona Barrie ....Virginia
Stepin Fetchit .... Scipio
Russell Simpson...Richards
Ronnie Crosby .... Harry
Jackie Cosbey ....Jackie
Almeda Fowler...Geraldine
Alden Chase ....Jack Hampton
Roy Watson ....Jefferson Davis
John Elliott ....Gen. Robert E. Lee
John Webb Dillon ....Gen. "Stonewall" Jackson
J.C. Fowler...Gen. Leonidas Polk
Andre Cheron...Gen. Beauregard
Based on *The House of Connelly* by Paul Green
Directed by Henry King
Screenplay by Reginald Berkeley

New Deal Rhythm Paramount. 1934.
This was a two-reel musical featurette, with Shirley in a bit part (serving as her screen test for Paramount).

Charles "Buddy" Rogers
Marjorie Main
Shirley Temple

Change of Heart Fox Film Corp. 1934.
Two couples get confused as to who loves whom. One girl deserts her friends for a rich man, but eventually realizes her mistake.

Janet Gaynor...Catherine Furness
Charles Farrell .... Chris Thring
James Dunn ....Mack McGowan
Ginger Rogers ....Madge Rountree
Beryl Mercer.. Harriet Hawkins
Gustav Von Seyffertitz ....Mr. Kreutzmann
Shirley Temple .... Shirley
Irene Franklin ....Greta Hailstrom
Fiske O'Hara ....T.P. McGowan
Drue Leyton ....Mrs. Mockby, Jr.
Mary Carr... Mrs. Rountree
Jane Darwell ....Mrs. McGowan
Kenneth Thomson ....Howard Jackson
Nella Walker..Mrs. Mockby
Barbara Barondess .... Phyllis Carmichael
Directed by John G. Blystone
Story by Kathleen Norris
Screenplay by Sonja Levine and James Gleason

Mandalay First National. 1934.

The heroine, played by Kay Francis, has two suitors. Suspense built up to where she murders the "bad guy" and gets away with it.

Kay Francis ....Tanya
Ricardo Cortez...Tony Evans
Warner Oland...Nick
Lyle Talbot..Dr. Gregory Burton
Ruth Donnelly ....Mrs. Peters
Reginald Owen ....Police Captain
Hobart Cavanaugh...Purser
David Torrence ....Captain
Rafaela Ottiano ....the Countess
Holliwell Hobbes...Col. Dawson Ames
Etienne Girardot...Mr. Abernathie
Lucien Littlefield...Mr. Peters
Bodil Rosing ....Mrs. Klienschmidt
Herman Bing ....Mr. Klienschmidt
Harry C. Bradley...Mr. Warren
James B. Leonig..Ram Singh
Shirley Temple ....Betty Shaw
Lillian Harmer ....Louisa Mae Harrington
Torben Meyer..Van Brinker
Directed by Michael Curtiz
Screenplay by Austin Parker and Charles Kenyon
Story by Paul Harvey Fox

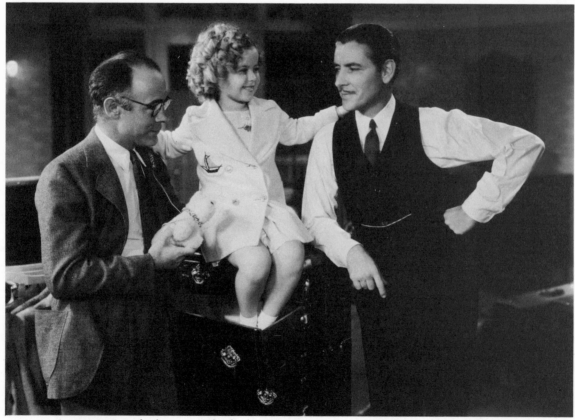

A promotional photo in which director Stephen Roberts (left) conspires with Shirley to put one over on Ronald Colman, who was preparing a scene for his film, *The Man Who Broke the Bank at Monte Carlo*.

Little Miss Marker Paramount. 1934.

Shirley is left by her father as a marker—security for a loan. He gambles the money, loses it and his life. The gambling establishment owner keeps the girl, makes her a real home.

Adolphe Menjou ....Sorrowful Jones
Dorothy Dell .... Bangles Carson
Charles Bickford ....Big Steve
Shirley Temple .... Miss Marker (Martha, Marky)
Lynne Overman ....Regret
Frank McGlynn, Sr. .... Doc Chesley
Jack Sheehan ....Sun Rise
Gary Owen..Grinder
Sleep 'n Eat ....Dizzy Memphis
Puggy White .... Eddie
Sam Hardy...Benny the Gouge
Tammany Young ....Buggs
Edward Earle ....Marky's father
John Kelly .... Sore Toe
Warren Hymer .... Canvas-Back
Frank Conroy .... Dr. Ingalls
James Burke...Reardon
Mildred Gover .... Sarah
Lucille Ward .... Mrs. Walsh
Crauford Kent..Doctor
Nora Cecil................................. Head of Home Finding Society
Directed by Alexander Hall
Produced by B.P. Schulberg
Story by Damon Runyon, published in *Colliers*, 1932

Suave Adolphe Menjou was tamed by Shirley in *Little Miss Marker*. Safety pins were part of his lessons on the care of little dolls.

Bottoms Up Fox Film Corp. 1934.

This musical introduced British musical star Pat Paterson to American viewers. She gets involved with gangsters between songs and dances.

Spencer Tracy .... Smoothie King
John Boles .... Hal Reede
Pat Paterson .... Wanda Gale
Herbert Mundin .... Limey Brock
Sid Silvers .... Spud Mosco
Harry Green .... Louis Wolf
Thelma Todd .... Judith Marlowe
Robert Emmett O'Connor .... Detective Rooney
Dell Henderson .... Lane Worthing
Suzanne Kaaren .... Secretary
Douglas Wood .... Baldwin
Directed by David Butler
Story by B.G. DeSylva, David Butler and Sid Silvers

Six-year-old Shirley is being prepared for her role in *Stand Up and Cheer* by the Fox studio make-up expert.

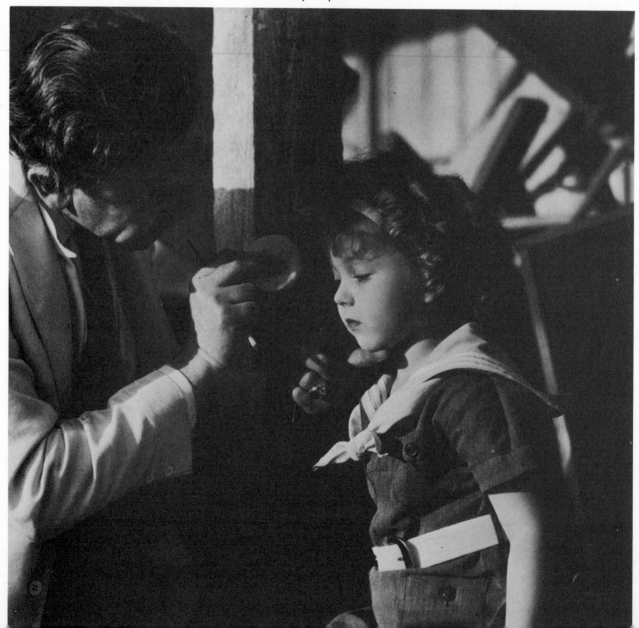

Stand Up and Cheer Fox Film Corp. 1934.

A Secretary of Amusement is appointed to the President's cabinet to cheer people with entertainment acts throughout America.

Warner Baxter ....Lawrence Cronwell
Madge Evans...Mary Adams
Shirley Temple ....Shirley Dugan
James Dunn ....Jimmy Dugan
Sylvia Froos..as herself
John Boles ....as himself
Arthur Byron ....John Harly
Ralph Morgan.................................Secretary to the President
Aunt Jemima (Tess Gardell) ....as herself
Mitchell & Durant ....Senators
Nick Foran...as himself
Nigel Bruce ....Dinwiddie
"Skins" Miller ....Hillbilly
Stepin Fetchit...as himself
Directed by Hamilton McFadden
Produced by Winfield Sheehan
Story idea by Will Rogers and Philip Klein
Screenplay by Lew Brown and Ralph Spence
Songs by Lew Brown and Jay Gorney
Costumes by Rita Kaufman

Shirley wore Girl Scout socks and her own special uniform to lead a section of the band for the *Stand Up and Cheer* finale. The drum was only for fun; she really used a baton.

(Above) In *Stand Up and Cheer*, Jimmy Dunn introduces Shirley with the song, "Baby Take a Bow." Shirley did just that—and everyone stood up and cheered. (Below) Madge Evans, once a child star herself, was cast as a supervisor of performing children in the same film.

Now I'll Tell Fox Film Corp. 1934.

Based on the life story of New York gangster Arnold Rothstein, as told by his wife. He risks her love and his life.

Spencer Tracy .... Murray Golden
Helen Twelvetrees .... Virginia
Alice Faye... Peggy
Robert Gleckler.. Mositer
Henry O'Neill .... Doran
Hobart Cavanaugh .... Freddie
G.P. Huntly, Jr.. Hart
Shirley Temple .... Mary Golden
Ronnie Crosbey .... Tommy Jr.
Ray Cooke... Traylor
Frank Marlowe .... Curtis
Clarence Wilson .... Davis
Barbara Weeks .... Wynne
Theodore Newton .... Joe
Vince Barnett .... Peppo
Jim Donlan .... Honey Smith
Directed by Edwin Burke

Baby, Take a Bow Fox Film Corp. 1934.

Shirley's gangster father, released from prison, tries to go straight. Shirley befriends a detective and gangster in pursuit of him.

Shirley Temple .... Shirley
James Dunn .... Eddie Ellison
Claire Trevor... Kay Ellison
Alan Dinehart .... Welch
Ray Walker .... Larry Scott
Dorothy Libaire .... Jane
Ralph Harolde.. Trigger Stone
James Flavin... Flannigan
Richard Tucker... Mr. Carson
Olive Tell .... Mrs. Carson
John Alexander .... Rag Picker
Directed by Harry Lachman
Produced by John Stone
Story by Philip Klein and E.E. Paramore, Jr.

Now and Forever Paramount. 1934.

Gary Cooper deserts his little girl, played by Shirley, for a life of crime. He returns to visit his daughter and tries to go straight for her sake.

Gary Cooper.. Jerry Day
Carole Lombard .... Toni Carstairs
Shirley Temple .... Pennie (Penelope Day)
Sir Guy Standing .... Felix Evans
Dog Buster .... Daschund
Charlotte Granville .... Mrs. J.H.P. Crane
Gilbert Emery.. James Higginson
Henry Kolker .... Mr. Clark
Tetsu Komai... Mr. Ling
Andre Dheron .... Inspector
Directed by Henry Hathaway
Story by Jack Kirkland and Melville Baker
Story adapted by Austin Parker

(Above) Spencer Tracy played role of a gangster in *Now I'll Tell*. Shirley is his daughter, Merry, in the film. On his other knee is Ronnie Crosbey.

(Below) A happy Shirley sits on Spencer Tracy's knee in a scene from *Now I'll Tell*. The other actors are Barbara Weeks, Ronnie Crosbey and Theodore Newton.

On the board, director Harry Lachman plots the entire day's shooting schedule for *Baby Take a Bow*. Actor Ray Walker is at the left and Stanley Scheur is in the rear.

Shirley poses here with Claire Trevor in a 1934 dramatic film, *Baby Take a Bow*.
Shirley's ballet dress set the style for dolls and little girls' dancing costumes.

In the film, *Baby Take a Bow* (also called *Here Is My Heart*), Shirley posed as Cupid with James Dunn, her favorite leading man.

Francis Carpenter, a former popular child-star himself, visited Shirley on her set when she was filming *Baby Take a Bow*.

To promote public safety, Shirley poses during the shooting of *Now and Forever* in an over-sized uniform. The National Safety Council was hoping the public would pay more attention to traffic regulations as a result of this promotional effort.

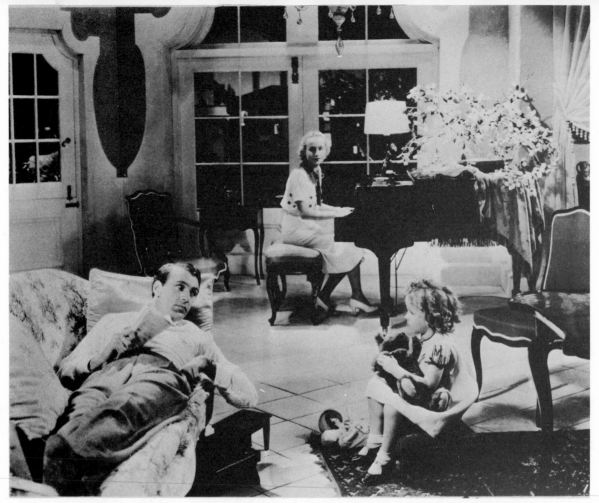

Carole Lombard, Gary Cooper's girlfriend in *Now and Forever*, plays the piano while Shirley plays with Grumpy. In the end, Shirley finds stolen pearls inside the stuffed animal.

Gary Cooper, who plays Shirley's Daddy, is a gangster in this 1934 movie, *Now and Forever*. The stolen goods were hidden in Grumpy, the teddy bear that Shirley is holding.

Bright Eyes Fox Film Corp. 1934.

When Shirley's mother is killed, there is a contest to see who will take the orphan. A rich old man wants her; so does his beautiful niece and a flyer friend of her dead father.

Shirley Temple ....Shirley Blake
James Dunn ....Loop Merritt
Jane Darwell ....Mrs. Higgins
Judith Allen ....Adele Martin
Lois Wilson ....Mary Blake (mother)
Charles Sellon ....Uncle Ned Smith
Walter Johnson ....Thomas
Jane Withers ....Joy Smythe
Theodore Von Eltz..................................J. Wellington Smythe
Dorothy Christy...Anita Smythe
Brandon Hurst ....Higgins
George Irving ....Judge Thompson
David O'Brien ....Airplane friend (later called "Tex")
Directed by David Butler and Edwin Burke
Screenplay by William Conselman

A high point of *Bright Eyes* was the Christmas Day party held in an airplane. Shirley sang "On the Good Ship Lollipop," a song with which she is still identified.

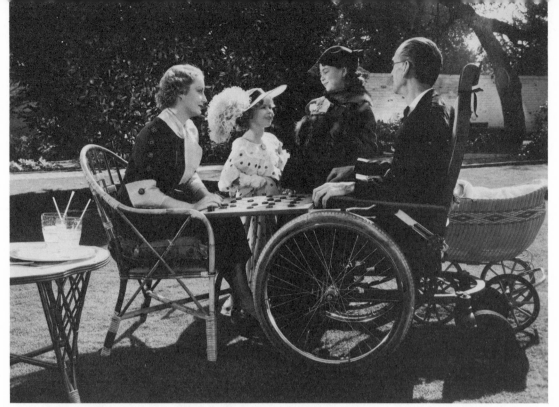

(Above) Judith Allen is playing checkers with Shirley and Jane Withers' uncle, Ned Smith (Charles Sellon). Sellon's big scene in *Bright Eyes* was coming down the stairs in his wheel chair. (Below) Lois Wilson was Mary Blake, and Shirley played her daughter in *Bright Eyes*. The scene was Christmas Eve. Shirley and her mother were discussing what Santa might bring.

The Little Colonel Fox Film Corp. 1934.

An old colonel's daughter marries against his will. When she returns to visit him with her daughter Shirley, she wins the old man's heart.

Shirley Temple .... Lloyd Sherman (the little colonel)
Lionel Barrymore .... Col. Lloyd
Evelyn Venable.................................... Elizabeth Lloyd Sherman
John Lodge ....Jack Sherman
Sidney Blackmer ....Swazey
Alden Chase .... Hull
William Burress .... Dr. Scott
David O'Brien .... Frank Randolph
Hattie McDaniel .... Mom Beck
Geneva Williams...Maria
Avonne Jackson ....May Lily
Nyanza Potts ....Henry Clay
Frank Darien... Nebler
Bill Robinson ....Walker
Directed by David Butler
Produced by B.G. De Sylva
Story by Annie Fellows Johnston
Screenplay by William Conselman

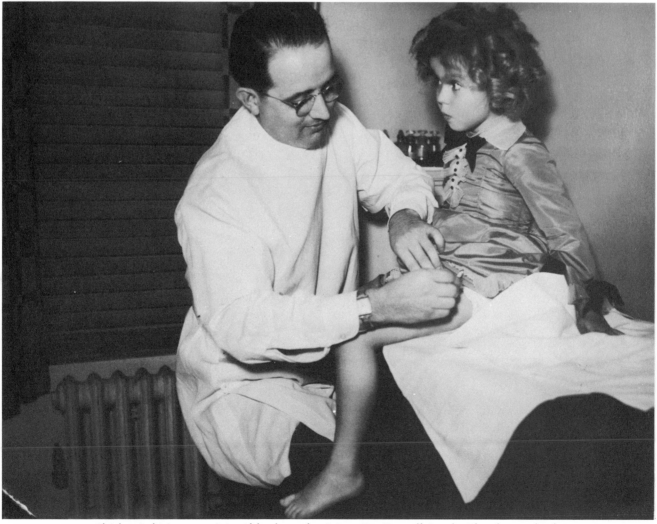

Shirley is being vaccinated by her physician, Dr. Russell Sands. The doctor had been taking care of her since she was five months old. The studio asked the doctor to wait until after the shooting of *The Little Colonel* before permitting the vaccination.

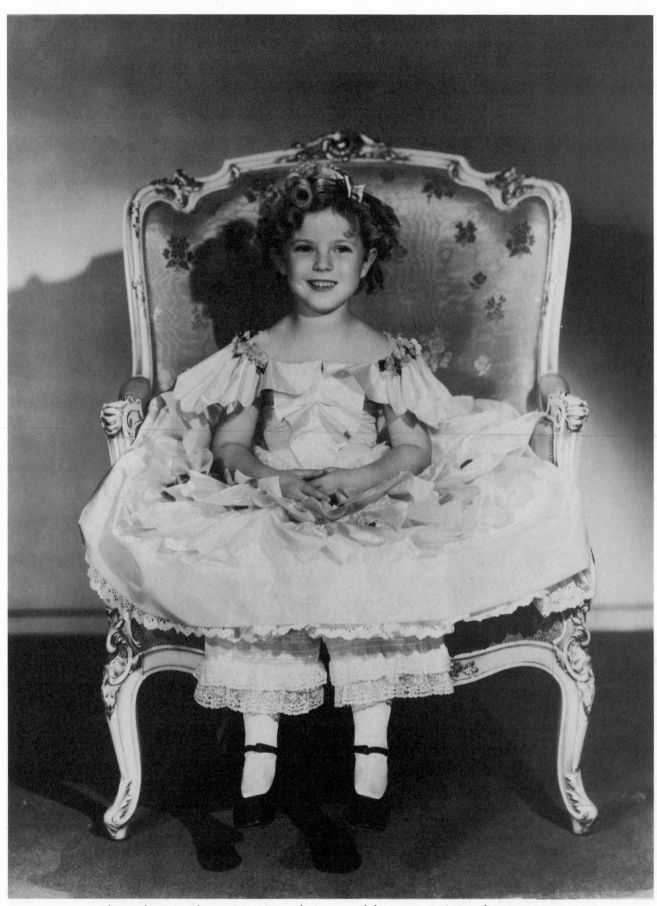

Shown here is a fantastic antique chair, one of the many antiques that were part of the set for *The Little Colonel*.

The concluding scene from *The Little Colonel* is this technicolor sequence called "A Pink Party." Here, Shirley is frowned upon by her grandfather, Lionel Barrymore. Evelyn Venable and John Lodge look on.

In *The Little Colonel*, Shirley returns to the deep South where her "Mama" grew up. She is joined here by Avonne Jackson and Nyanza Potts to re-enact a baptism.

Tap dancer Bill Robinson joins Shirley in a "dance up-and-down-the-steps" routine. The sequence was used in *The Little Colonel*.

1935 FILMS

Our Little Girl Fox Film Corp. 1935.

A busy doctor neglects his wife. They are about to break up, so their little girl runs away. Their worry and love for her reunite them.

Shirley Temple ....Molly Middleton
Rosemary Ames..Elsa Middleton
Joel McCrea ....Dr. Donald Middleton
Lyle Talbot...Rolfe Brent
Erin O'Brien-Moore ....Sarah Boynton
Poodles Hanneford ....Circus performer (clown, himself)
Margaret Armstrong .... Amy
Rita Owin..Alice
Leonard Carey .... Jackson
J. Farrell MacDonald ....Mr. Tramp
Jack Baxley .... Leyton
Directed by John Robertson
Produced by Edward Butcher
Story by Florence Leighton Pfalzgraf, *Heaven's Gate*
Screenplay by Stephen Avery, Allen Rivkin and Jack Yellen

Curly Top Fox Film Corp. 1935.

Orphaned Shirley and her sister, much too cheerful and musically talented for the orphanage, are rescued by a trustee who adopts Shirley and finally marries her sister.

Shirley Temple ....Elizabeth Blair (Betsy)
John Boles, Edward Morgan, orphanage trustee
Rochelle Hudson ....Mary Blair, Betsy's sister
Jane Darwell ....Mrs. Denham
Rafaela Ottiano ....Mrs. Higgins
Esther Dale .... Aunt Genevieve
Arthur Treacher ....Morgan's butler
Directed by Irving Cummings
Produced by Winfield Sheehan
Story by Jean Webster, *Daddy Long Legs*
Story adapted by William Conselman
Screenplay by Patterson McNutt and Arthur Beckhard

The Littlest Rebel Twentieth Century-Fox. 1936.

Shirley plays a blackface scene in this classic drama, a departure from her other screen images of a blonde curly top.

Shirley Temple ....Virginia Houston Cary (Virgie)
John Boles ....Confederate Captain Herbert Cary
Jack Holt ....Union Colonel Morrison
Karen Morley...Mrs. Cary
Bill Robinson ....Uncle Billy, Cary servant
Guinn Williams ....Sergeant Dudley
Willie Best .... James Henry
Frank McGlynn, Sr..President Lincoln
Bessie Lyle... Mammy
Hannah Washington ....Sally Ann
Directed by David Butler
Produced by Darryl F. Zanuck
Associate producer B.G. De Sylva
Story by Edward Peple, based on *The Littlest Rebel*
Screenplay by Edwin Burke and Harry Tugend

The movie was *Our Little Girl*. Rosemary Ames was Shirley's mother Elsa. (Top) Mother and daughter welcome the man of the house who comes home bearing gifts. (Bottom) Director John Robertson is trying to find out why Shirley is in the doll's bed instead of on the set preparing for her next scene.

(Above) Boys and girls working as extras on the set of *Our Little Girl* were so fascinated by young Shirley that they could not stay away from her even when a scene was not being shot. Here, they watch her as she writes a note to her stage mother, Rosemary Ames. (Below) Outdoor scenes for the 1935 movie were shot on location at Sherwood Lake, at a spot called "Heaven's Gate." Shirley and her doctor father (Joel McCrae) enjoy a lovely picnic on a beautiful summer day.

(Top) In one of the sequences in *Curly Top*, Shirley and actor Siegfried Rumann take the same pose as in the world famous painting, "The Helping Hand." (Bottom) In *Curly Top*, John Boles, an orphanage trustee, was very much interested in Shirley's sister, played here by Rochelle Hudson. John first adopted both sisters and then fell in love and married Rochelle.

Shirley is dressed as a woman of 65 in the Fox movie, *Curly Top*. In this film, Shirley played four different ages: age 6, age 16, age 21 and age 65.

Rebel captain Herbert Carey (John Boles) is Shirley's father in *The Littlest Rebel*. Here, he succeeds in convincing her to be brave as he prepares to leave for the front.

In this scene from *The Littlest Rebel*, Karen Morley is attended to by a Yankee intruder (Guinn Williams) after she fell down the stairs. Shirley tries, unsuccessfully, to hide her identity behind blackface make-up.

To avoid the wrath of the advancing Union army in *The Littlest Rebel*, Shirley dons blackface. Between scenes, she poses for the director of the film, David Butler.

(Above) A behind-the-scenes view of the shooting of *The Littlest Rebel*, as Shirley commands her troops. This Civil War drama was produced by Darryl F. Zanuck.

(Below) In *The Littlest Rebel*, a charming minuet is broken up by an announcement that the war is starting. Shirley protests having to leave her partner, Freddie McManus, with whom she had been dancing.

1936 FILMS

Captain January Twentieth Century-Fox. 1936.

Orphan Shirley is rescued from a shipwreck by a lighthouse keeper. A truant officer insists on better surroundings and schooling, and relatives are finally located.

Shirley Temple	Star
Guy Kibbee	Captain January
June Lang	Mary Marshal
Slim Summerville	Captain Nazro
Buddy Ebsen	Paul Rogers
Sara Haden	Agatha Morgan
Jane Darwell	Eliza Croft
Jerry Tucker	Cyril Morgan
Nella Walker	Mrs. John Mason
George Irving	John Mason
James Farley	Deputy sheriff
Si Jenks	Old sailor
John Carradine	East Indian
Mary McLaren	Nurse at aunt's home
Billy Benedict	Messenger boy

Directed by David Butler
Produced by Darryl F. Zanuck
Associate producer B.G. De Sylva
Story by Laura E. Richards, *Captain January*
Screenplay by Sam Hellman, Gladys Lehman and Harry Tugend

The Poor Little Rich Girl Twentieth Century-Fox. 1936.

Shirley's rich father is too busy to spend time with her. She becomes a radio star and it evolves into just the advertising needed for her father's soap company.

Shirley Temple	Barbara Barry
Alice Faye	Jerry Dolan
Gloria Stuart	Margaret Allen
Jack Haley	Jimmy Dolan
Michael Whalen	Richard Barry (father)
Sara Haden	Collins
Jane Darwell	Woodward
Claude Gillingwater	Simon Peck
Henry Armetta	Tony
Arthur Hoyt	Percival Gooch
John Wray	Flagin
Paul Stanton	George Hathaway
Charles Coleman	Stebbins
John Kelly	Ferguson
Tyler Brooks	Dan Ward
Mathilde Comont	Tony's wife
Leonard Kilbrick	Freckles
Dick Webster	Soloist
Bill Ray	Announcer
Gayne Whitman	Announcer (assumed)

Directed by Irving Cummings
Produced by Darryl F. Zanuck
Associate producer B.G. De Sylva
Story suggested by Eleanor Gates and Ralph Spence
Screenplay by Sam Hellman, Gladys Lehman, and Harry Tugend

Slim Summerville and Guy Kibbee join Shirley in an operatic song in an interesting scene from *Captain January*.

Jerry Tucker and Shirley look at each other suspiciously in *Captain January*, the film which co-starred Guy Kibbee and Buddy Ebsen.

Shirley is practicing a hula-hula dance on the soft sands of the Pacific beach for her role in *Captain January*.

A beautiful opera frock was worn by Shirley in the 1936 production, *Captain January*. The film was highly successful and had an extended run.

(Left) Shirley sneaks out of her affluent home and is happy playing in the street with the monkey of organ grinder Henry Armetta. Others with her in *Poor Little Rich Girl* were Alice Faye and Jack Haley (not shown in this scene).

(Below) A behind-the-scenes view of a boom— a glorified crane on top of which the cameraman perched himself to get this shot of Shirley, Alice Faye and Jack Haley in the Twentieth Century-Fox production, *Poor Little Rich Girl*.

Shirley played the part of a pampered rich girl in *Poor Little Rich Girl*. This photo, with Michael Whalen, was used for promotion.

Dimples Twentieth Century-Fox. 1936.

Grandfather, played by Frank Morgan, was not providing the proper atmosphere for Dimples, and a rich lady seeks to adopt the child. But Dimples needs love more than atmosphere.

Shirley Temple ....Sylvia Dolores Appleby (Dimples)
Frank Morgan .... Professor Appleby
Helen Westley..Mrs. Caroline Drew
Robert Kent...Allen Drew
Delma Byron..Betty Loring
Astrid Allwyn .... Cleo Marsh
Stepin Fetchit...Cicero
Berton Churchill...Colonel Loring
Paul Stanton ....Mr. St. Clair
Julius Tannen .... Hawkins
John Carradine...Richards
Herman Bing ....Proprietor
Billy McClain ....Rufus
The Hall Johnson Choir...Choir
Jack Clifford .... Uncle Tom
Betty Jean Hainey ....Topsy
Arthur Aylesworth .... Pawnbroker
Greta Meyer ....Proprietor's wife
Leonard Kilbrick, Warner Weidler, Walter Weidler, and George Weidler .... Children's band
Jesse Scott and Thurman Black ....the Two Black Dots
Directed by William A. Seiter
Produced by Darryl F. Zanuck
Associate producer Nunnally Johnson
Screenplay by Arthur Sheekman and Nat Perrin
Dances staged by Bill Robinson

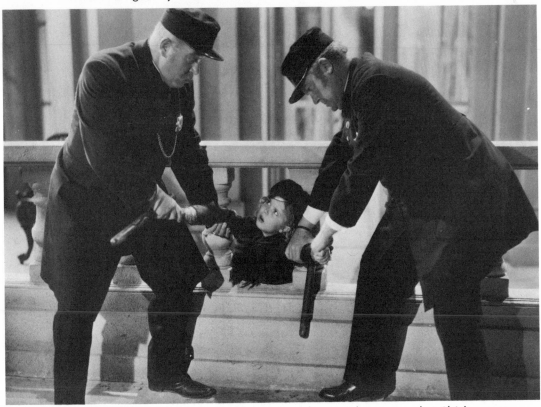

In the film, *Dimples*, the boys in the band made a quick getaway, but Shirley got caught. The police were actually after her grandfather.

Here, Shirley is taking some time out to have a little fun with assistant director Booth McCracken during the shooting of *The Bowery Princess*. The name of the movie was later changed to *Dimples*.

(Top) Shirley, playing the part of little Eva in *Uncle Tom's Cabin*, is alarmed when the police are about to pick up Frank Morgan who has attempted to disguise himself. The scene is from *Dimples*.

(Bottom) Shirley Temple and Frank Morgan pose for a scene in the same film.

Stowaway Twentieth Century-Fox. 1936.

The orphaned daughter of missionaries in China is befriended by a playboy, who later adopts her. Shirley imitates Ginger Rogers and Fred Astaire in a dance scene.

Shirley Temple ....Ching-Ching, daughter of missionaries
Robert Young ....Tommy Randall
Alice Faye...Susan Parker
Eugene Pallette .... The Colonel
Helen Westley.......................................Mrs. Hope
Arthur Treacher .... Atkins
J. Edward Bromberg ....Judge Booth
Astrid Allwyn ....Kay Swift
Allan Lane .... Richard Hope
Robert Greig...Captain
Jayne Regan...Dora Day
Julius Tannen ....First Mate
Willie Fung ....Chang
Phillip Ahn ....Sun Lo
Paul McVey .... Second Mate
Helen Jerome Eddy ....Mrs. Kruikshank
William Stack .... Alfred Kruikshank
Honorable Wu ....Latchee Lee
Directed by William A. Seiter
Produced by Darryl F. Zanuck
Associated producers B.G. De Sylva, Earl Carroll, and Harold Wilson
Story by Sam Engel
Screenplay by William Conselman, Arthur Sheekman, and Nat Perrin

Stowaway included this scene in which Shirley beat out all her competitors in a theatre contest by doing an imitation of Al Jolson singing "Mammy."

Mrs. Elise Deal, Shirley's personal dressmaker, puts the finishing touches on the costume to be worn in *Stowaway*. Shirley's costumes were usually designed by Gwen Wakeling.

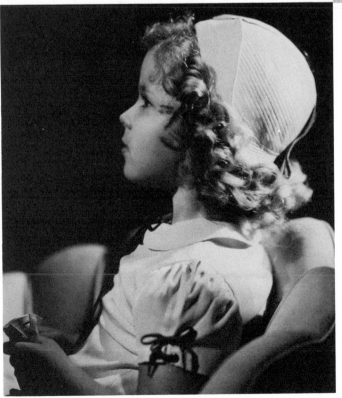

An unusual profile pose from the Twentieth Century-Fox film, *Stowaway*.

Shirley had just lost another tooth, and she looks soberly through the porthole. The scene is from *Stowaway*, in which she co-starred with Robert Young.

1937 FILMS

Wee Willie Winkie Twentieth Century-Fox. 1937.

While visiting her grandfather in India, Shirley befriends a prisoner who is the leader of rebel natives. When they attack her grandfather's troops, Shirley goes to beg for peace.

Shirley Temple ....Priscilla Williams
Victor McLaglen .... Sergeant MacDuff
C. Aubrey Smith...Colonel Williams
June Lang .... Joyce Williams
Michael Whalen ....Lt. Brandes, called Coppy
Cesar Romero .... Khoda Khan
Constance Collier .... Mrs. Allardyce
Douglas Scott .... Private Mott
Gavin Muir .... Capt. Bibberbeigh
Willie Fung ....Mohammet Dihu
Brandon Hurst .... Bagby
Lionel Pape.. Major Allardyce
Clyde Cook ....Pipe Major Sneath
Lauri Beatty ....Elsie Allardyce
Lionel Braham.............................Major Gen. Hammond
Mary Forbes .... Mrs. MacMonachie
Cyril McLaglen..Corporal Tummel
Jack Pennick ....Soldier guard and
Shirley's military instructor offstage

Directed by John Ford
Produced by Darryl F. Zanuck
Associate producer Gene Markey
Story by Rudyard Kipling
Screenplay by Ernest Pascal and Julien Josephson

Heidi Twentieth Century-Fox. 1937.

Orphaned Shirley goes to stay with her grandfather high in the Alps. Her aunt kidnaps her and takes her to Frankfurt. Shirley tries to return to the Alps, while the grandfather hunts for her.

Shirley Temple .... Heidi
Jean Hersholt .... Adolph Kramer
Arthur Treacher ....Andrews
Helen Westley .... Blind Anna
Pauline Moore ....Elsa
Thomas Beck .... Pastor Schultz
Mary Nash ....Fraulein Rottenmeier
Sidney Blackmer.. Herr Sesemann
Mady Christians ....Aunt Dete
Sig Rumann ....Police Captain
Marcia Mae Jones ....Klara Sesemann
Delmar Watson ....Peter, the goat boy
Egon Brecher .... Innkeeper
Christian Rub..Baker
George Mumbert ....Organ grinder
Directed by Allan Dwan
Produced by Darryl F. Zanuck
Associate producer Raymond Griffith
Story by Johanna Spyri
Screenplay by Walter Ferris and Julien Josephson

Shirley Temple says good-bye to 1936 as she looks forward to 1937, a year in which two of her famous classics would be produced: *Heidi* and *Wee Willie Winkie*.

June Lang, who played Shirley's mother in *Wee Willie Winkie*, spanks her daughter for getting into the petunia bed and ruining the flowers.

In this scene from *Wee Willie Winkie*, Constance Collier argues with C. Aubrey Smith as Shirley looks on in amazement.

Shirley has words with her grandfather, the colonel (C. Aubrey Smith), in the 1937 production of Rudyard Kipling's *Wee Willie Winkie*. Sgt. MacDuff, standing behind her, was played by Victor McLaglen.

Jack Rennick instructs Shirley in the proper military stance as she enacts her role of a private in the Queen's Army in *Wee Willie Winkie*.

Here, in the same dress that she wore at the *Wee Willie Winkie* premiere, Shirley prepares to cut the cake for a March of Dimes celebration in honor of President Franklin Delano Roosevelt. Eddie Cantor shook the hand that cut the cake.

In a scene from *Heidi*, Shirley leans on the shoulder of a friend to do a dream sequence. It was followed by a Dutch dance that became so popular that it was copied in many public school programs.

In the rear seat of the sleigh, Marcia Mae Jones, Shirley and Sidney Blackmer are enjoying this outside scene while filming *Heidi* for Twentieth Century-Fox.

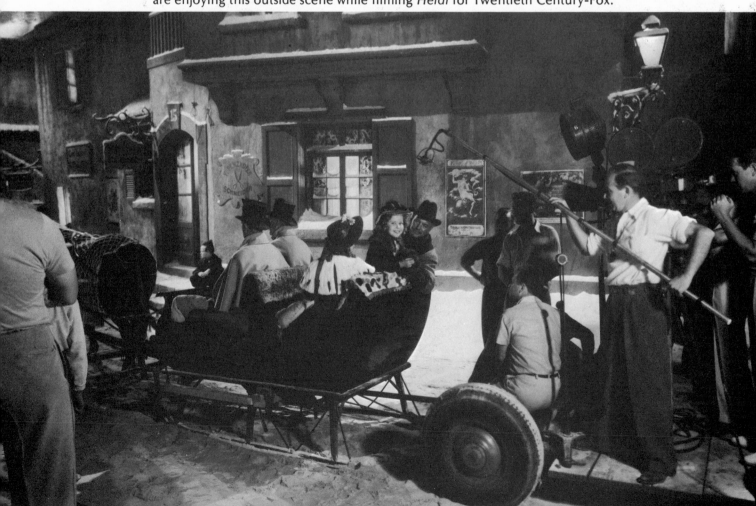

Jean Hersholt plays Shirley's grandfather in this scene from *Heidi*. He is preparing a bite to eat and she attempts to befriend him.

People were always anxious to meet Shirley. Here, Iving Berlin (left) brings his daughter, Mary Ellin, to meet Shirley and director Allan Dwan on the set of *Heidi*.

1938 FILMS

Rebecca of Sunnybrook Farm Twentieth Century-Fox. 1938.
Shirley, unwanted by her stepfather, goes to live on her aunt's farm. When she sings on the radio, the stepfather suddenly recognizes her value.

Shirley Temple .... Rebecca Winstead
Randolph Scott .... Anthony Kent
Jack Haley .... Orville Smithers
Gloria Stuart .... Gwenn Warren
Phyllis Brooks .... Lola Lee
Helen Westley .... Aunt Miranda Wilkins
Slim Summerville .... Homer Busby
Bill Robinson .... Aloysius
Raymond Scott Quintet .... as themselves
Alan Dinehart .... Purvis
J. Edward Bromberg .... Dr. Hill
Dixie Dunbar .... Receptionist
Paul Hurst .... Mug
William Demarest .... Henry Kipper
Ruth Gillette .... Melba
Paul Harvey .... Cyrus Bartlett
Clarence Hummel Wilson .... Jake Singer
Sam Hayes, Gary Breckner, Carroll Nye .... Radio announcers
Franklin Pangborn .... Hamilton Montmarcy
Directed by Allan Dwan
Produced by Darryl F. Zanuck
Associate producer Raymond Griffith
Story suggested by Kate Douglas Wiggin
Screenplay by Karl Tunberg and Don Ettlinger
Cinematography by Arthur Miller

Just Around the Corner Twentieth Century-Fox. 1938.
Shirley's widowed father is a maintenance man at a hotel, where his love lives in the penthouse. Shirley helps get her father a better job and a wife.

Shirley Temple .... Penny Hale
Charles Farrell .... Jeff Hale
Joan Davis .... Kitty
Amanda Duff .... Lola
Bill Robinson .... Corporal Jones
Bert Lahr .... Gus
Franklin Pangborn .... Waters
Cora Witherspoon .... Aunt Julia Ramsby
Claude Gillingwater, Sr. .... Samuel G. Henshaw
Bennie Bartlett .... Milton Ramsby
Hal K. Dawson .... Reporter
Charles Williams .... Candid cameraman
Eddie Conrad .... French tutor
Tony Hughes and Orville Caldwell .... Henshaw's assistants
Marilyn Knowlden .... Gwendolyn
Directed by Irving Cummings
Produced by Darryl F. Zanuck
Associate producer David Hemptstead
Story by Paul Gerard Smith
Screenplay by Ethel Hill, J.P. McEvoy and Darrell Ware

Shirley is doing a dance with Bill Robinson in *Rebecca of Sunnybrook Farm*. They dropped metallic blackberries into the bucket to add flavor to their soft-shoe routine.

(Above) Gloria Stewart was cousin Gwen in *Rebecca of Sunnybrook Farm*. Here, after showing Shirley around the farm, she tells her more about farm life.

(Below) Shirley removes an egg from the dye as she prepares for an Easter scene in *Rebecca of Sunnybrook Farm*.

Bert Lahr, Joan Davis and Bill Robinson join Shirley Temple in this comedy-dance routine from *Just Around the Corner*.

In this scene from *Just Around the Corner*, Shirley insisted that Bennie Bartlett confess to his mother about the fight he had just had in which his clothes were torn and his eye was blackened.

Shirley is having a lively conversation with Charles Farrell, who played her father in *Just Around the Corner*.

Little Miss Broadway Twentieth Century-Fox. 1938.

    Shirley, living at a hotel for theatrical performers, is in a battle with her friends against a rich neighbor who objects to their noise. A court appearance saves them from eviction.

Shirley Temple	Betsy Brown
George Murphy	Roger Wendling
Jimmy Durante	Jimmy Clayton
Phyllis Brooks	Barbara Shea
Edna Mae Oliver	Sarah Wendling
George Barbier	Fiske
Edward Ellis	Pop Shea
Jane Darwell	Miss Hutchins
El Brendel	Ole
Donald Meek	Willoughby Wendling
Patricia Wilder	Flossie
Claude Gillingwater, Sr.	Judge
George and Olive Brasno	as themselves
Charles Williams	Mike Brody
Charles Coleman	Simmons
Russell Hicks	Perry
Brian Sisters	as themselves for specialty number
Brewster Twins	Guests
Claire DuBrey	Miss Blodgett
Robert Gleckler	Detective
C. Montague Shaw	Miles
Frank Dae	Pool
Clarence Hummel Wilson	Scully
Eddie Collins, Syd Saylor, Jerry Colonna, Heinie Conklin	Members of the band
Ben Weldon	Taxi driver

Directed by Irving Cummings
Produced by Darryl F. Zanuck
Original story by Harry Tugend and Jack Yellen

Shirley is leading two of her girlfriends at the orphanage in a happy song in the film, *Little Miss Broadway*. The two girls are the Brian sisters. Shirley is happy because she is about to leave the orphanage for a real home.

Shirley joined George Murphy (later to become a senator from California) in the 1938 production, *Little Miss Broadway*. They danced atop model buildings amid flashing skylines.

(Left) Phyllis Brooks, as Barbara, puts "Little Miss Broadway" to bed in the film by the same name. Shirley's curls were carefully pinned as in her everyday, regular fashion. Fans got a rare glimpse of the *real* Shirley in this film.

(Below) Jimmy Durante joins Shirley in a "big apple" dance in a scene from *Little Miss Broadway*. The presiding judge was Claude Gillingwater, Sr., always the perfect crab.

1939 FILMS

The Little Princess Twentieth Century-Fox. 1939.

Shirley's father indulges her in a princess-style life, but he goes to war and is reported dead. A girls' school mistress makes her a servant. She finds that her father is still alive—in a hospital.

Shirley Temple ....Sara Crewe
Richard Greene..Geoffrey Hamilton
Anita Louise..Rose
Ian Hunter .... Capt. Crewe
Cesar Romero .... Ram Dass
Arthur Treacher ....Bertie Minchin
Mary Nash .... Amanda Minchin
Sybil Jason ....Becky
Miles Mander .... Lord Wickham
Marcia Mae Jones .... Lavinia
Beryl Mercer.. Queen Victoria
Deidre Gale .... Jessie
Ira Stevens... Ermengarde
E.E. Clive ....Mr. Barrows
Keith Kenneth..Bobbie
Will Stanton and Harry Allen ....Grooms
Holmes Herbert, Evan Thomas, Guy Bellis ....Doctors
Kenneth Hunter ....General
Lional Braham ....Colonel
Directed by Walter Lang
Produced by Darryl F. Zanuck
Associate producer Gene Markey
Based on the story by Frances Hodgson Burnett
Screenplay by Ethel Hill and Walter Ferris

Susannah of the Mounties Twentieth Century-Fox. 1939.

Shirley, the sole survivor of an Indian massacre, is rescued by mounted police, and she helps them improve relations with the Indians.

Shirley Temple .... Susannah Sheldon
Randolph Scott ....Monty (Inspector Angus Montague)
Margaret Lockwood...Vicky Standing
Martin Good Rider .... Little Chief
J. Farrell MacDonald ....Pat O'Hannegan
Maurice Moscovich .... Chief Big Eagle
Moroni Olsen .... Supt. Andrew Standing
Victor Jory ....Wolf Pelt
Lester Matthews .... Harlan Chambers
Leyland Hodgson... Randall
Herbert Evans ....Doctor
Jack Luden ....Williams
Charles Irwin ....Sergeant McGregor
John Sutton ....Corporal Piggot
Chief Big Tree.. Chief
Directed by William A. Seiter
Produced by Darryl F. Zanuck
Associate producer Kenneth Macgowan
Story based on the book by Muriel Denison
Adapted by Fidel La Barba and Walter Ferris
Screenplay by Robert Ellis and Helen Logan

Arthur Treacher does a little jig with Shirley in the 1939 film, *The Little Princess*.

(Above) When Shirley's father, in *The Little Princess*, lost his money, the mistress of the boarding school made her work as a servant. She sneaks out to hunt for her father and finally finds him.

(Below) In *The Little Princess*, Shirley first sits on a throne and watches the graceful ballerinas. Enthralled, she leaves her throne and joins the company in some simple steps.

In this scene from *The Little Princess*, Shirley fantasizes that she is a *real* princess. She is shown here with Arthur Treacher.

In the 1939 film, *Susannah of the Mounties*, Shirley survives a massacre, and is rescued by Mountie Randolph Scott.

2
THE MIDDLE YEARS

Shirley as a bride in 1945.

In and Out of the Teen Years

Westlake School for Girls was not an average school, by any measurement. It was a whole new world and 12-year-old Shirley was naturally curious.

The school exposed Shirley Temple to a wide variety of girls, but most were from her general social class. They were not awed by her status as a star. These were not like the girls at the studio who wanted to get close to Shirley in order to advance in their film careers.

When Shirley celebrated her 12th birthday, she learned from her mother that it was in fact her 13th. She was as surprised as was the public. The correction had to be announced officially because *The World Book* had entered her date of birth as 1929 instead of 1928.

Reporters tried to delve into Shirley's private life, but found the door on her privacy securely closed. Shirley and her mother became very private people. Thus, it was never definitely learned what type of relationship existed between mother and daughter. Was it pleasant? Was it casual? Did Mrs. Temple continue to dictate her daughter's tastes, habits and career?

So many people admired the Temples and looked up to them with reverence that it was practically impossible to live truly private lives.

The termination of the Fox contract in 1940 certainly did not end Shirley Temple's career. By December of that year she had signed a contract with MGM. Her first picture was to be *Kathleen*, the story of a motherless girl.

Work was not begun until Shirley had her vacation in school and had her tonsils out. Her salary of $100,000 annually allowed for eight radio broadcasts a year, a

In 1940, at the age of 12, Shirley is given a royal welcome on her second visit to Honolulu.

guarantee of 40 weeks of work, billing that was either top or equal to that of any other top star, reasonable lodging at the studio for Shirley and her mother, plus no requirement (because of her young age) to join the Screen Actors Guild. A judge approved the contract.

The contract was cause for numerous rumors to circulate. There was talk of her appearing in a Mickey Rooney-Judy Garland picture, and also as a participant, after a gradual write-in, in the successful Hardy series starring Rooney and Garland.

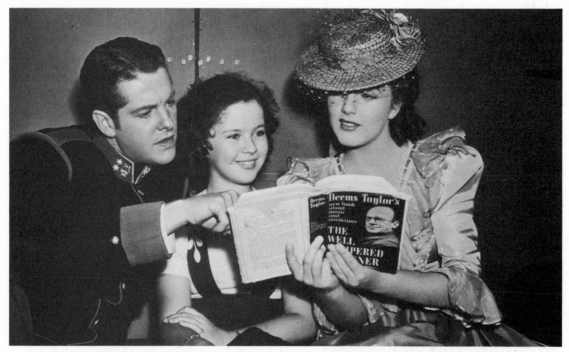

Posing with a new Deems Taylor book about music and musicians, Deanna Durbin and Robert Cummings, who in 1940 were filming *Spring Parade*, visited Universal to pose with Shirley for a publicity shot.

While the film *Kathleen*, which co-starred Herbert Marshall, followed the main feature at most theaters, it was considered a solid picture, and her talent was rated very high.

Preparing for a screen comeback in 1941, Shirley joins Olsen and Johnson in this publicity shot to promote their film, *Hellzapoppin*. Kneeling is Nick Castle, her dancing coach.

Nearly everyone was struck with the beauty of her maturing figure and face. Columnists began to comment on her overall beauty and bearing. The color of her hair was constantly commented upon in nearly every writeup. Whether red, streaked or black, everyone seemed continually surprised that it had not remained blonde and curly.

She was delayed in getting back to Westlake that fall because she had to finish *Kathleen*. The movie completed, she returned, taking along all 14 dresses that had been designed for the film thus augmenting her own personal wardrobe. She let her hair grow to its natural color which was deep brown with reddish spots interspersed.

During December of 1941, she did four weekly radio shows called, "Shirley Temple Time," for Elgin watches. The major actors who were her guest stars were Warner Baxter, Robert Young, Lionel Barrymore and Humphrey Bogart. Two days after the first broadcast, on December 7, 1941, Pearl Harbor was attacked by the Japanese.

The involvement of the United States in World War II was of great personal concern to Shirley because her brother George had enlisted in the Marines in 1940. It was two weeks before she learned he was safe. She also learned that he was listening to her broadcasts, and so on her last show, as an unrehearsed bit that issued from the heart, she ended with a whispered, "Hello George." Her other brother, Jack, married in 1942 and he, too, entered the service.

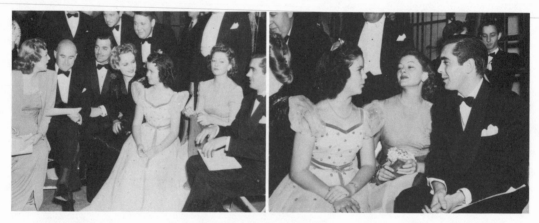

When Shirley went on radio to assist the Greek War Relief effort, she was helped by a great supporting cast. Among those in the group above are Melvyn Douglas, Charles Laughton, Clark Gable and Carole Lombard. Seated beside Shirley are Myrna Loy and Tyrone Power.

During the United China Relief Fund Drive, Shirley contributed by signing up to care for three children. She had contributed earlier, in 1941, to the Greek War Relief Fund by joining fellow workers Clark Gable, Myrna Loy, Ronald Colman, Bob Hope, Tyrone Power and Carole Lombard in an *America Calling* broadcast at Grauman's Chinese Theatre. The fund-raising event resulted in contributions of $142,000.

At Westlake, the war was the reason for military drill being introduced, and Shirley worked herself up to the rank of drill sergeant and, then, finally lieutenant.

In her next film, *Miss Annie Rooney*, with William Gargan and Guy Kibbe, she was cast as a typical teenager of the period. She jitterbugged quite well (although in real life she preferred the dreamy dances instead of wild ones), got her first screen kiss on the cheek, and spoke in the teen-jive jargon that was very much in vogue at Westlake.

Shirley began a new weekly radio show of her own on March 4, 1942, called *Junior Miss*. She received $3,000 for each show. The program was renewed after the first 13 weeks.

She followed this up by signing with David O. Selznick at United Artists, in 1943, to do *Since You Went Away*, a serious war film co-starring Claudette Colbert and Jennifer Jones. She turned in an outstanding performance. She won the hearts of every teenager and serviceman from coast to coast and all over the world. Soldiers overseas wrote for pictures, preferring her to the pin-up queens that normally were plastered on the walls of military barracks. Some wrote to her and included pictures of her that they had taken from captured or dead Japanese and German soldiers. Servicemen considered her like a kid sister or like the girl-next-door who was young enough to still be single by the time they came home.

An informal shot celebrating the filming of *Since You Went Away*. Shown left to right are director John Cromwell, Hattie McDaniel, Shirley, Claudette Colbert and David O. Selznick.

Squadron 111 at El Toro Marine Corps Air Station, in Southern California, adopted her as a kid sister. She visited the base, stopping to eat chocolate cake and chatting with the boys, even trying on a few jackets. She was also a favorite at the Hollywood Canteen, sometimes dancing with a hundred or so fellows, and often just letting them talk, or giving them autographs.

At one military hospital, where the servicemen were mostly amputees, she visited to express her appreciation, realizing that their sacrifice was, in part, for her and all her fellow Americans. There were many hospital visits. She found that they treasured her visits and that because of her fame, her presence was to them a source of great comfort. She was trying to say to them, by her presence, "thanks . . . we care."

In 1944, Shirley went to Canada to assist in the official opening of the Seventh Canadian War Loan Drive. Here, Prime Minister Mackenzie King welcomes her. He later wrote how very attractive and natural she was.

The war effort kept her quite busy. She visited hospitals in New York, and helped with bond drives. She visited Canada for its Victory Loan campaign in October, 1944, speaking in Toronto in English, and in Quebec in French. She also appeared in Canada at the launching of eight ships. A C-54 transport was named the Shirley Temple and she was glad to pose with the huge plane.

A postal worker in Hollywood reported Shirley got more mail from servicemen than 75% of the pin-up girls. Her weekly mail ran into several thousands, filling bag after bag at the post office. She was every serviceman's kid sister.

In a 1944 Selznick film, *I'll Be Seeing You*, she again portrayed the "sweetheart of the service" or "kid sister" image. Shirley believed such roles were important.

In addressing a New York Herald Tribune forum on the motion picture industry, she suggested that there was a great need for more films dealing with the problems of servicemen, because films like the one she had done served young men away from home as a great morale booster.

In 1944, Shirley takes a trip to New York to do some shopping and sightseeing. In Bonwit Teller, a salesgirl, Finette McCarthy, shows Shirley the latest style in hats.

Shirley wasn't exactly a typical teenager in her next role, the 1945 *Kiss and Tell* comedy by F. Hugh Herbert. Some people felt it detracted from her screen and private image. To be associated with all the innuendoes of an illegitimate baby, even though it ended happily, they argued, was harmful to her career. During the filming of *Kiss and Tell*, Shirley had to kiss some 100 strangers before the final take was okayed. One of the sequences showed her selling kisses to 22 servicemen. Reporters asked her if she had had any practice before the rehearsals. She demurely parried the question with an, "Of course not."

When her parents found out that she had begun to learn to drive a girl friend's car without a driver's permit, they stopped her—explaining that if anything happened it would create unfavorable publicity all over the country, and, even worse, possibly encourage other teenagers to emulate her (bad) example.

By the time *Kiss and Tell* was released, Shirley had graduated from Westlake. At the senior luncheon, Shirley did not try very hard to hide the diamond engagement ring that she had received from Sgt. John Agar. She admitted that she was still too young to settle down, and promised to wait several years before marrying John. All over America, people suddenly felt older as they began thinking of Shirley's approaching marriage. Teenagers used it as an excuse to pressure their own parents to permit engagements and marriages at younger ages.

Shirley looks lovely, happy and proud. It is June, 1945, and it's graduation day for her and her classmates at Westlake School for Girls.

When John was expected to be sent overseas, Shirley and John changed their minds about waiting and were married at the start of his 10-day leave. It was a church wedding with all the traditional trimmings. The date was September 19, 1945. Shirley was only 17 years old, and the war in Japan had just ended.

About 10,000 fans crowded outside the church. Shirley invited many of her friends, including prop men and other studio personnel.

Film producers were quick to notice the tall, good-looking groom, age 24, and eagerly inquired as to his acting ability potential. They were quite aware of the publicity that had come his way as a result of his marriage to Shirley.

Sgt. Agar went back to camp, but not overseas. Shirley's visits with him were followed by reporters and photographers.

Almost 17 years old, Shirley announces her engagement to 24-year-old Sgt. John Agar—6' 3'' tall, blond, handsome and a physical education instructor at March Field during World War II. The year is 1945.

Kiss and Tell was a success, and Shirley's next film role was in *Honeymoon for Two*, a story which called for wearing a wedding gown. She made several of the covers of movie magazines, and on the inside they carried features of her advice and opinions on marriage.

An 18-year-old Shirley Temple gave advice in the May, 1946 *Movieland* magazine, to youthful actress-star Margaret O'Brien, which was valid and appropriate to everyone. In the article, she told Margaret not to measure people by their popularity and station in life, but "to consider the humanity and feeling exhibited by each of greater importance." She warned not to be too eager to pry into the affairs of others, nor to divulge your own too freely. "Study and become as well informed as possible," she said, "because as an actress you'll meet a great many outstanding people, including scientists, statesmen, writers and artists, and you'll want to speak and understand their language."

Shirley also commented on the importance of learning to share the many gifts to be received with hospitals and charities. "Regard the honors, the gifts, and the luxuries as privileges, not just as things that are your due," she said. "But enjoy what you have thoroughly. You do work hard and deserve enjoyment."

The marriage of this handsome couple, Mr. and Mrs. John Agar, shown with daughter Susan, was officially announced to be "on the rocks" in October, 1949 —just one month after this family picture was taken in the yard of their Hollywood home.

Meanwhile, husband John was discharged from the service, and the couple was now living together. Shirley had completed *The Bachelor and the Bobby Soxer* with Cary Grant, in 1946, and *That Hagen Girl* with Ronald Reagan, released in 1947. She was now to do a picture with her husband as a co-star. It was called *Fort Apache* and featured John Wayne and Henry Fonda. It gave fans a better look at her husband who played the role of Lt. O'Rourke. He also appeared in a supporting role in another movie, *Adventure in Baltimore*, which featured Shirley and Robert Young.

Shirley was one of the world's most publicized mothers when she gave birth to a beautiful baby girl, Linda Susan. The sad news of her pending divorce that followed in less than two years was likewise widely publicized by the press. When news of the divorce, which became final in 1950, hit the newspapers, some 30,000 people wrote to her, and most expressed their sympathy and regret.

Shirley commented only briefly about the divorce in an article in *Motion Picture* magazine. "My first marriage was a mistake," she said abruptly. "I am not afraid to think about it or to remember it, but I would rather not discuss it. It was no one's fault. It just should never have happened."

So it was. It ended and it was over. It involved the emotions of many people, hurting some, shocking some, and drawing criticism especially from the columnists who lived by Hollywood gossip. Perhaps the hardest part for Shirley was the problem of not being left alone with her own inner feelings. The public was always digging and questioning.

Shirley did not remain single for long. Late in December of 1950, she became Mrs. Charles Black in a private ceremony at the home of his parents in Monterey, California. The following spring Charles was recalled to duty with the navy and they headed east. Their first baby was born at a naval hospital—a son named Charles.

They moved to Palo Alto, California, when Charles' job was settled there. A daughter, Lori, was born, and Shirley was a busy housewife. She and Charles found time to take daughter Susan to the White House to visit President Eisenhower. But, otherwise, Shirley avoided the limelight. When her daughter Susan caught press notices for a kindergarten pantomime, she withdrew the child from the play. *Time* and *Newsweek* picked up the story.

As Shirley's children grew older and took up less of her time, she began to take a more active interest in community affairs. She participated in the Multiple Sclerosis effort as a volunteer worker in 1954, adding to her scope of activity the Peninsula Children's Theater Association in 1955. She followed this in 1956 with volunteer work at the Stanford Children's Convalescent Hospital Auxiliary, and later devoted time to the Mid-Peninsula's Children's Health Council.

All these activities provided Shirley with much satisfaction. It was a different kind of world for Shirley, for it was so far removed from film-making and show business. She was now Mrs. Charles Black: housewife and community affairs volunteer worker.

1940 FILMS

The Blue Bird Twentieth Century-Fox. 1940.
Shirley and her brother prove, while searching for the "blue bird of happiness," that happiness is at home—not in a far-off exotic place.

Shirley Temple ....Mytyl
Spring Byington...Mummy Tyl
Nigel Bruce .... Mr. Luxury
Gale Sondergaard ....Tylette the cat
Eddie Collins...Tylo the dog
Sybil Jason .... Angela Berlingot
Jessie Ralph ....Fairy Berylune
Helen Ericson...Light
Johnny Russell .... Tyltyl
Laura Hope Crews ....Mrs. Luxury
Russell Hicks...Daddy Tyl
Cecilia Loftus .... Granny Tyl
Al Shean ....Grandpa Tyl
Gene Reynolds..Studious boy
Leona Roberts ....Mrs. Berlingot
Stansey Andrews .... Wilheim
Dorothy Dearing .... Cypress
Frank Dawson ....Caller of Roll
Claire DuBrey ....Nurse
Sterling Holloway .... Wild Plum
Thurston Hall...Father Time
Edwin Maxwell...Oak
Herbert Evans and Brandon Hurst .... Footmen
Dewey Robinson ....Royal Forester
Keith Hitchcock ....Major Domo
Buster Phelps ....Boy Inventor
Tommy Taker and Dorothy Joyce ....Lovers
Billy Cook .... Boy Chemist
Scotty Beckett, Juanita Quigley and Payne Johnson ....Children
Ann Todd...Little sister
Diane Fisher .... Little girl
Directed by Walter Lang
Produced by Darryl F. Zanuck
Associate producer Gene Markey
Story by Maurice Maeterlinck
Screenplay by Ernest Pascal

Gale Sondergaard (right) plays the part of a cat reincarnated, and Laura Hope Crews plays the part of Mrs. Luxury. The film was the 1940 production, *The Blue Bird*.

Above and below are two scenes in which Shirley carries the blue bird in the film based on Maurice Maeterlinck's famous fantasy, *The Blue Bird*. Spring Byington, Nigel Bruce and Gale Sondergaard were featured in the film.

Young People Twentieth Century-Fox. 1940.

Shirley and her parents leave show business to settle on a farm. Their neighbors reject them until they rescue children in a storm.

Shirley Temple .... Wendy
Jack Oakie .... Joe Ballantine
Charlotte Greenwood .... Kit Ballantine
Arleen Whelan .... Judith
George Montgomery .... Mike Shea
Kathleen Howard .... Hester Appleby
Minor Watson .... Dakin
Frank Swann .... Fred Willard
Frank Sully .... Jeb
Sara Edwards .... Mrs. Stinchfield
Mae Marsh .... Marie Liggett
Irving Bacon .... Otis
Charles Halton .... Moderator
Arthur Aylesworth .... Doorman
Olin Howland .... Station Master
Billy Wayne .... Stage Manager
Harry Tyler .... Dave
Darryl Hickman .... Tommy
Shirley Mills .... Mary Ann
Diane Fisher .... Susie
Bobby Anderson .... Jerry Dakin
Directed by Allan Dwan
Produced by Harry Joe Brown
Screenplay by Edwin Blum and Don Ettlinger

Loud-mouthed Charlotte Greenwood is cast to compete with vaudevillian Jack Oakie in the 1940 film, *Young People*. Shirley had to exert herself considerably to make her voice heard.

A dramatic scene from the Twentieth Century-Fox production of *Young People*. Arleen Whelan (above) played the part of Judith. George Montgomery co-starred in the film.

1941 FILMS

Kathleen Metro-Goldwyn-Mayer. 1941.
  Shirley's wealthy father has little time for her. A psychologist comes to study her and stays to marry her father.

Shirley Temple ....Kathleen Davis
Herbert Marshall ....Father, John Davis
Laraine Day .... Dr. A. Martha Kent
Gail Patrick .... Lorraine Bennett
Felix Bressart.. Mr. Schoner
Nella ·Walker...Mrs. Farrell
Lloyd Corrigan .... Dr. Montague Foster
Guy Bellis ....Jarvis
Wade Boteler... Policeman
Charles Judels .... Manager
Else Argal ....Maid
Margaret Bert ....Margaret
Joe Yale .... Sign poster
Directed by Harold S. Bucquet
Produced by George Haight
Based on the story by Kay Van Riper
Screenplay by Mary C. McCall, Jr.

In the 1941 MGM movie, *Kathleen*, motherless Shirley is befriended by psychologist Laraine Day.

1942 FILMS

Miss Annie Rooney United Artists. 1942.
 At a rich boy's party, Shirley's father explodes an invention and creates a horrible scene, but nevertheless, this gets him a job with the boy's father.

Shirley Temple .... Annie Rooney
William Gargan .... Tim Rooney
Guy Kibbee .... Grandpop
Dickie Moore .... Marty
Peggy Ryan .... Myrtle
Roland DuPree .... Joey
Gloria Holden .... Mrs. White
Jonathan Hale .... Mr. White
Mary Field .... Mrs. Metz
George Lloyd .... Burns
Jan Buckingham .... Madam Sylvia
Selmer Jackson .... Mrs. Thomas
June Lockhart .... Stella Bainbridge
Charles Coleman .... Sidney
Edgar Dearing .... Policeman
Virginia Sale .... Myrtle's mother
Shirley Mills .... Audrey Hollis
Directed by Edwin L. Marin
Produced by Edward Small
Screenplay by George Bruce

Mary Pickford and Shirley, in Hollywood in 1943, are pictured together for the first time. Mary was just 15 when she scored her first film success in *The New York Hat*, and here, Shirley at 15, is about to play her first dramatic role in *Since You Went Away*.

(Above) Shirley is joined by Dickie Moore, who tries to follow her in a dance routine in the *Miss Annie Rooney* film. Also in the cast were William Gargan, Guy Kibbee and Peggy Ryan.

(Below) In *Miss Annie Rooney*, Shirley rode home in this jalopy belonging to her boyfriend, Roland Dupree. This was her first "grown-up" role.

1943 FILMS

Since You Went Away United Artists. 1943.

Shirley's father goes to war, and Claudette Colbert mothers her and her sister through the problems of loneliness, love and bereavement.

Claudette Colbert	Anne Hilton
Jennifer Jones	Jane
Shirley Temple	Bridget (Brig)
Hattie McDaniel	Fidelia
Jane Devlin	Gladys Brown
Lloyd Corrigan	Mr. Mahoney
Monty Woolley	Col. Smollet
Agnes Moorehead	Emily Hawkins
Joseph Cotten	Lt. Anthony Willett
Robert Walker	Corp. William G. Smollett, II
Jackie Moran	Johnny Mahoney
Guy Madison	Harold Smith, a sailor
Lionel Barrymore	Clergyman
Craig Stevens	Danny Williams
Albert Basserman	Dr. Sigmund Gottlieb Golden
Nazimova	Zofia Kislowska, a welder
Keenan Wynn	Lt. Solomon

Directed by John Cromwell
Produced by David O. Selznick
Based on the book by Margaret Buell Wilder
Screenplay by David O. Selznick

I'll Be Seeing You United Artists. 1943.

Ginger Rogers, on leave from prison, meets Joseph Cotten, who is fighting battle shock. They fall in love. Shirley reveals Ginger's prison background.

Ginger Rogers	Mary Marshall
Joseph Cotten	Zachary Morgan
Shirley Temple	Barbara Marshall (Mary's cousin)
Spring Byington	Mrs. Marshall
Tom Tully	Mr. Marshall
Chill Wills	Swanson
Dave Harris	Lt. Bruce
Kenny Bowers	Sailor on the train
Olin Howlin	Hawker
Dorothy Stone	Salesgirl
John James	Paratrooper
Eddie Hall	Charlie Hartman
Joe Haworth	Sailor in coffee shop
Jack Carr	Counterman
Bob Meredith	Soldier-father on train
Robert Dudley	YMCA hotel attendant
Margaret Bert	Mother of boys
Mickey Laughlin, Hank Tobias and Gary Gray	Boys outside theater
Earl W. Johnson	Dog owner

Produced by William Dieterle
Directed by Dore Schary
Story by Charles Martin

Jennifer Jones (center) and Claudette Colbert sympathize with Shirley in this dramatic scene when the man of the family had to go off to war. The movie was *Since You Went Away*.

Oddly enough, it was Shirley's 16th birthday when Monty Woolley presented her with this Walter Pitkin volume. Shirley was on the Selznick set shooting *I'll Be Seeing You*.

(Above) *Since You Went Away* was a tense drama written and produced by David O. Selznick. Shirley is shown here with Claudette Colbert.

(Below) In *I'll Be Seeing You*, Shirley gets into the middle of a love affair, and is the source of much trouble between Ginger Rogers and Joseph Cotten. Spring Byington and Tom Tully were Shirley's parents in the film.

Shirley greets tennis star Francisco "Pancho" Segura in September, 1944, at the National Amateur Tennis championship tournament held in Forest Hills, New York. Together, they made radio broadcasts to audiences in many Latin American countries.

Shirley Temple, in 1944, is rewarded for her tireless effort during World War II. She christens a giant C-54 transport, named in her honor at Santa Monica, California.

Shirley is posing with Walter Winchell, in 1944, at the Stork Club in New York. This was Winchell's home-away-from-home where he picked up most of the juicy morsels for his gossip column.

Shirley, at 16, spent time in New York City making publicity appearances. She is shown appearing with Rudy Vallee on NBC.

1945 FILMS

Kiss and Tell Columbia. 1945.

Shirley's family gets into a feud with the family of her best friend, who is secretly married to her brother. Her sister-in-law visits an obstetrician, and Shirley keeps it a secret.

Shirley Temple ....Corliss Archer
Jerome Courtland..Dexter Franklin
Walter Abel .... Mr. Archer
Katharine Alexander ....Mrs. Archer
Robert Benchley................................Uncle George, a chaplain
Porter Hall.. Mr. Franklin
Edna Holland ....Mrs. Franklin
Virginia Welles ....Mildred Pringle
Tom Tully .... Mr. Pringle
Mary Phillips..Mrs. Pringle
Darryl Hickman ....Raymond Pringle
Scott McKay ....Private Jimmy Earhart
Scott Elliott ....Lenny Archer
Directed by Richard Wallace
Produced by Sol C. Siegel
Story by F. Hugh Herbert
Screenplay by F. Hugh Herbert

In *Kiss and Tell*, Shirley sold linen at a charity bazaar. She was doing poorly, so she convinced her boyfriend, Jerome Courtland, to help by making a purchase. Later, she repays him with a kiss.

In the 1945 Columbia comedy, *Kiss and Tell*, Shirley turns up at the studio in her own slacks . . . But the scene called for *shorts*! After a series of conferences, the director allowed the scene to be played in this unscheduled outfit.

Newlyweds John Agar and Shirley Temple pose for some publicity shots immediately after their wedding in September, 1945. (Inset) Shirley's mother (standing to her left) joins the reception line.

1946 FILMS

Honeymoon RKO. 1946.

Shirley goes to Mexico City to meet her soldier fiance on leave, but their planned marriage and honeymoon are delayed by many obstacles.

Shirley Temple ....Barbara Olmstead
Franchot Tone.. David Flanner
Guy Madison ....Phil Vaughn
Lina Romay...Raquel Mendoza
Gene Lockhart ....Prescott
Corinna Mura ....Senora Mendoza
Grant Mitchell .... Crenshaw
Julio Vilareal .... Senor Mendoza
Manual Arvide ....Registrar
Jose R. Goula ....Doctor Diego
Directed by William Keighley
Produced by Warren Duff
Based on the story by Vicki Baum
Screenplay by Michael Kanin

The Bachelor and the Bobby Soxer RKO. 1946.

Shirley gets a crush on playboy artist Cary Grant, but he escapes her clutches by falling in love with her sister.

Cary Grant... Dick
Myrna Loy .... Margaret
Shirley Temple ....Susan
Rudy Vallee .... Tommy
Ray Collins ....Bemish
Harry Davenport .... Thaddeus
Johnny Sands .... Jerry
Don Beddoe .... Tony
Lillian Randolph .... Bessie
Veda Ann Borg ....Agnes Prescott
Dan Tobin .... Walters
Ransom Sherman...Judge Treadwell
William Bakewell...Winters
Irving Bacon .... Melvin
Ian Bernard ....Perry
Carol Hughes..Florence
William Hall .... Anthony Herman
Gregory Gay ....Maitre d'Hotel
Directed by Irving Reis
Produced by Dore Schary
Story by Sidney Sheldon
Screenplay by Sidney Sheldon

Shirley and Guy Madison get a chance to enjoy Mexico City where *Honeymoon* is to be shot. At the last moment, plans were changed and a new location was selected.

In *Honeymoon*, Shirley imagines that she is in love with Franchot Tone, the American vice-consul who is trying to straighten out complications that have developed between Shirley and her groom, Guy Madison.

Student Shirley Temple is mesmerized by lecturer Cary Grant in *The Bachelor and the Bobby Soxer*. Here, she and her classmate, Johnny Sands, listen attentively. Later, Shirley follows Cary to his apartment.

In *The Bachelor and the Bobby Soxer*, Cary Grant and Rudy Vallee end up competing for the affections of Shirley.

1947 FILMS

That Hagen Girl Warner Bros.-First National. 1947.

Town gossipers question who Shirley's parents were, and when society people snub her, she attempts suicide.

Shirley Temple .... Mary Hagen
Ronald Reagan .... Tom Bates
Dorothy Peterson .... Mother, Minta Hagen
Charles Kemper .... Jim Hagen
Rory Calhoun .... Ken Freneau
Jean Porter .... Sharon Bailey
Nella Walker .... Molly Freneau
Winifred Harris .... Selma Delaney
Ruth Robinson .... Cora
Lois Maxwell .... Julia Kane
Conrad Janis .... Mary's dance date, Dewey Koons
Penny Edwards .... Christine Delaney
Harry Davenport .... Judge Merrivale
Directed by Peter Godfrey
Produced by Alex Gottlieb
Based on the novel by Edith Roberts
Screenplay by Charles Hoffman

In this scene from *The Hagen Girl*, Rory Calhoun is the stereotyped tall, dark, and handsome boy of good breeding dancing with Shirley. In the end, Ronald Reagan plays up to her.

1948 FILMS

Fort Apache Argosy Pictures Production, RKO release. 1948.
   Shirley's soldier-father objects to her boyfriend. The father orders a war party against the Indians, and only the boyfriend escapes to bring news of the massacre back to the fort.

John Wayne	Captain York
Henry Fonda	Col. Thursday
Shirley Temple	Philadelphia Thursday
Pedro Armendariz	Sergeant Beaufort
Ward Bond	Sergeant O'Rourke
George O'Brien	Capt. Collingwood
John Agar	Lt. O'Rourke
Victor McLaglen	Sergeant Mulachy
Anna Lee	Mrs. Collingwood
Irene Rich	Mrs. O'Rourke
Miguel Inclan	Chief Cochise
Dick Foran	Sergeant
Jack Pennick	Sergeant
Guy Kibbee	Post surgeon
Grant Withers	Indian agent
Mae Marsh	Post resident

Directed by John Ford
Presented by John Ford and Merian C. Cooper
Story by James Warner Bellah, based on "Massacre" in *Saturday Evening Post*
Screenplay by Frank S. Nugent

Adventure in Baltimore RKO. 1948.
   Shirley, crusading for women's votes, ends up in jail. Her painting rocks 1908 Baltimore and nearly gets her minister father fired.

Robert Young	Dr. Sheldon
Shirley Temple	Dinah Sheldon
John Agar	Tom Wade
Albert Sharpe	Mr. Fletcher
Josephine Hutchinson	Mrs. Sheldon
Charles Kemper	Mr. Steuben
Johnny Sands	Gene Sheldon
John Miljan	Mr. Eckert
Norma Varden	H.H. Hamilton
Carol Brannan	Bernice Eckert
Patti Brady	Sis Sheldon
Gregory Marshall	Mark Sheldon
Patsy Creighton	Sally Wilson

Directed by Richard Wallace
Produced by Richard H. Burger
Screenplay by Lionel Houser

(Top) A beautiful shot of the *Fort Apache* cast, which included Irene Rich, Victor McLaglen, Henry Fonda, Annalee, George O'Brien, Shirley Temple and Dick Foran. Shirley's father (Henry Fonda) was in charge of the military post in *Fort Apache*. (Bottom) While visiting her father, she meets John Agar who becomes her boyfriend.

(Top) In the 1949 RKO release, *Adventure in Baltimore*, Dad (Robert Young) was the pastor. He is shown here between Shirley and Josephine Hutchinson. Her husband, John Agar, is on the extreme right. (Bottom) Shirley and Josephine Hutchinson in another scene from *Adventure in Baltimore*. Josephine, holding the boxing gloves, tries to offer her some sage advice.

1949 FILMS

Mr. Belvedere Goes to College Twentieth Century-Fox. 1949.

As a journalism student desperate for a scoop, Shirley clashes with Mr. Belvedere, who shuns publicity.

Clifton Webb .... Lynn Belvedere
Shirley Temple .... Ellen Baker
Tom Drake .... Bill Chase
Alan Young .... Avery Brubaker
Jessie Royce Landis .... Mrs. Chase
Kathleen Hughes .... Kay Nelson
Taylor Holmes .... Dr. Gibbs
Alvin Greenman .... Corny Whittaker
Paul Harvey .... Dr. Keating
Barry Kelly .... Griggs
Bob Patten... Joe Fisher
Lee MacGregor .... Hickey
Helen Westcott .... Marian
Jeff Chandler .... Pratt
Clancy Cooper .... McCarthy
Eevelynn Eaton .... Sally
Judy Brubaker .... Barbara
Kathleen Freeman .... Babe
Lotte Stein .... Marta
Peggy Call .... Jean Auchincloss
Ruth Tobey .... Nancy
Elaine Ryan .... Peggy
Pattee Chapman .... Isabelle
Joyce Otis... Fluffy
Lonnie Thomas... Davy
Reginald Sheffield .... Prof. Ives
Colin Campbell .... Prof. Lindley
Katherine Lang .... Miss Cadwaller
Isabel Withers .... Mrs. Myrtle
Arthur Space.. Instructor
Directed by Eliott Nugent
Produced by Samuel G. Engel
Story by Gwen Davenport (based on character from *Sitting Pretty*)
Screenplay by Richard Sale, Mary Loos and Mary McCall, Jr.

The Story of Seabiscuit Warner Bros. 1949.

Story about the famous race horse. Shirley's father trains race horses and her fiance rides Seabiscuit to victory.

Shirley Temple .... Margaret O'Hara
Barry Fitzgerald .... Shawn O'Hara
Lon McCallister..Ted Knowles
Rosemary De Camp .... Mrs. Charles S. Howard
Donald MacBride .... George Carson
Pierre Watkin.. Charles S. Howard
William Forrest... Thomas Miltford
"Sugarfoot" Anderson .... Murphy
Wm. J. Cartledge.................................... Jockey George Woolf
Seabiscuit via genuine footage
Directed by David Butler
Screenplay by John Taintor Foote

(Above) Clifton Webb barges into Shirley's room in *Mr. Belvedere Goes to College*. After many troubles, the movie ends happily with Shirley marrying Tom Drake.

(Below) Shirley is shown with Clifton Webb, a freshman, in *Mr. Belvedere Goes to College*. All Shirley wanted was a publicity scoop, while all he wanted was to avoid publicity so he could stay in college.

When Shirley made her comeback, she returned to Fox to make *Mr. Belvedere*. At the time, there were many parties given and pictures taken. She is posing with Darryl F. Zanuck.

Lon McCallister was Shirley's sole love interest in *The Story of Seabiscuit*, filmed in 1949. He, however, divided his attention between her and his horses.

As a nurse in the film, *The Story of Seabiscuit*, Shirley had to learn an Irish brogue, and she learned it well. Here, she enjoys a laugh with her father (Barry Fitzgerald).

A Kiss for Corliss United Artists, independently produced by Enterprise Studios at General Service. 1949.

Shirley has an imaginary love affair, details of which are written in her diary and found by her excitable father.

Shirley Temple ....Corliss Archer
David Niven... Kenneth Marquis
Tom Tully .... Mr. Archer
Virginia Welles ....Mildred
Darryl Hickman .... Dexter Franklin
Robert Ellis ....Raymond Archer
Richard Craig.. Taylor
Directed by Richard Wallace
Produced by Colin Miller
Story based on character created by F. Hugh Herbert
Screenplay by Howard Dimsdale

Virginia Welles and Tom Tully in a scene from *A Kiss For Corliss*. Shirley drives Tully mad with her bubble-blowing juvenile antics.

3
THE LATER YEARS

Although Shirley had already given up her acting career, a fan calls on her in this 1954 pose.

A Return to Public Life

Shirley absented herself from show business for seven years. She was lured back to the entertainment world in January, 1957, by the offer of a national television show. It was called *Shirley Temple's Storybook*.

The show consisted of fairy tales, mostly adaptations of classical stories, some of which were completely rewritten.

Shirley, then approaching her 29th birthday, was a beautiful host. On each program, she introduced the program, narrated, and sang the theme song always wearing a different, elegant gown. Often, she also starred in the presentation.

Shirley commuted from home to work each day. She wanted to be away from her husband and children as little as possible. The show, which was carried on NBC, competed with the Disney Hour which ran at the same time. Nevertheless, it received considerable publicity and was successful. *Redbook* magazine gave her a cover, and an inside story, both in one month. *Life* magazine followed suit with a cover and an inside story. *Newsweek* previewed the show on September 29, and described how Shirley's children were making their acting debuts in the series: Susan at 10, Charles Jr. at 6, and Lori at 4. Charles had a speaking part which he did while climbing a pole to herald the prince's arrival, and he was paid $570.00. His sisters, who did not have speaking roles, received only $80.00.

Shirley Temple's Storybook was lavishly produced, and at all times featured top stars, even on those occasions when Shirley herself played the lead.

Critics were not of one opinion in their critical evaluation. Some were unhappy with her acting. Some loved everything about the shows. Others objected to the rewriting

145

that the traditional stories underwent, and felt that they strayed too far from the original.

Shirley began a new television series on NBC on September 18, 1960, called *The Shirley Temple Show*, again in competition with Disney which appeared in the same time slot. The opening show was *The Land of Oz*, in which Shirley played both Princess Ozma and a small boy, Tip. The stars included Jonathan Winters, Sterling Holloway, Arthur Treacher and Agnes Morehead. Most people expected it to be the *Wizard of Oz* and were baffled by the differences.

Later shows that were presented included *The Terrible Clockman* and *Onawandah*. The program attempted to bring to the public old favorites as well as lesser known stories by beloved authors.

This new program received considerable publicity, as did her earlier TV effort. More than a dozen covers of television magazines as well as magazine sections of newspapers devoted stories to the show.

Shirley's return to television was good enough reason for the Ideal Toy Company to come out with a new Shirley Temple doll. Daughter Susan carried a 36-inch version of the new Shirley doll in Macy's traditional big Thanksgiving Day parade in New York in 1959. New Shirley Temple coats and dresses were quickly licensed, and Shirley's personal appearances at various department stores to promote them attracted mobs to the stores.

Shirley returned to Palm Springs in 1959 to reign as queen of that Southern California desert resort city's 23rd annual Circus Days—something she had done several times when she was a child and a teenager.

She made several special appearances on television during that period. She sang and danced on Dinah Shore's Chevrolet show in 1958, and joined Art Carney and Janis Paige in a Chevrolet TV special. She celebrated her 35th birthday while filming Red Skelton's television opener for the fall, 1963 season. Shirley turned hobo for one scene with Red, sporting a dirty face in one of the most interesting moments of her show business career.

In June of 1963, Shirley hosted a special television show on KGO-TV in San Francisco. It was called, "Shirley Temple Presents Young America on Stage." Geared to focus in on the problems of juveniles, the two-hour show included a few ex-Mouseketeers and many amateurs. Its purpose was to encourage the youth of America to make the most of every opportunity that comes their way.

Shirley became more and more involved with various social and charitable functions. She worked on behalf of the Junior League. She helped in the 1963 benefit premiere of *It's a Mad, Mad, Mad World* for San Francisco Press Club's scholarship fund. She posed being arrested or accosted by two Keystone Kop-style pressmen. She helped with the KQUD auction in June, 1963, to raise funds for San Francisco's educational TV channel. She also assisted the station during the two years that followed.

She and her husband joined singer John Raitt for a pre-*Carousel* dinner, and made news when she shook her fist at novelist Niven Busch for his take-off on California politicians.

Shirley recorded a cassette tour for the U.S. museum and art gallery celebrity series of guided lectures. She donated wood carvings for a charity auction; received, in 1964, a special award for her contributions to Bay area educational TV; and even performed for the Junior League as a mermaid, during one of its fund-raising efforts.

In November of 1964, she received another award for outstanding service to the California youth from the state's Teachers' Association. Dr. Max Rafferty, California's top educator, gave her special praise in his newspaper column after she took her stand in opposition to the film *Night Games*. She protested the presentation of *Night Games* (which she said was "pornography for profit"), at the 10th annual San Francisco International Film Festival in 1966. Some adults had banned it at the Venice

Shirley took advantage of her two TV series (1957 and 1960) to present her line of Shirley Temple dolls, manufactured by Ideal Toy Co. She made department store appearances to help promote the dolls.

Film Festival. *McCall's* magazine published Shirley's opinions titled "Sex at the Box Office" in its January, 1967 issue.

In 1952, when her brother George left a sports and wrestling career, the victim of a nerve-damaging affliction, Shirley became interested in Multiple Sclerosis and its fund-raising drive. In 1954, she worked for the KNXT-TV MS Give-a-Thon, with Mickey Rooney as master of ceremonies. She participated in the *San Francisco Examiner's* "Encounter" series, in 1963, to discuss MS with neurologist Dr. Knox Finley.

When the National Multiple Sclerosis Society held its fifth anniversary with a fashion show in 1969 at the Sheraton-Park Hotel in Washington, D.C., Shirley was honorary chairman, and Mrs. Richard Nixon was a gracious patron. Shirley, who had been national chairman of the Hope Chest fund campaign in 1960, presented the MS Bronze Hope Chest Award to Don Hearn of the *Washington News* in 1969.

Shirley was back at the capital a couple of months later at a presentation of an award to President Nixon. The occasion marked the start of a five-year program to raise 10 million dollars for MS research. She took home Nixon's autograph to her father, who was 81.

ABC and 20th Century-Fox approached Shirley about another television show. A pilot for a half-hour situation comedy television series, "Go Fight City Hall," was filmed in 1965. She was to play the role of an unmarried social worker working for a welfare agency in San Francisco.

The pilot didn't materialize into a series because Shirley decided not to go ahead with it. Instead, she was off on a vacation trip to Europe with her husband, then an Ampex vice-president. After visiting London for six days, she went to Russia to confer with Soviet doctors regarding their progress in combating multiple sclerosis.

While in Russia, she also did some sightseeing. She was disappointed when she was not allowed to visit former premier Khrushchev who had invited her when he was in Hollywood in 1959. She visited a Moscow film theatre, saw the Russian cosmonauts welcomed home in Red Square, and taped a brief television speech.

In the fall of 1965, Shirley and daughter Lori went to Vienna to attend a medical conference and gain further information on MS. She was also working to set up an international organization on MS for research and the exchange of information. They stopped over in London where Shirley addressed a conference on MS. Newspapers pointed out how admirable it was that Shirley's only purpose, in all her travels, had been to gather information that might help others, and was not at all motivated to add to her own glory or adulation.

At the time, when Shirley completed an MS fund-raising tour in the U.S. just before her trip to Europe, husband Charles was named to the Advisory Board of the University of Santa Clara's School of Business.

In July of 1967, California's Governor, Ronald Reagan, the former actor who had appeared in a movie with Shirley when she was a child star, appointed her public representative on the Advisory Hospital Council, and Charles was appointed to serve on the Governor's task force. Both she and Charles had been active in Republican politics. They had attended the 1964 Republican National Convention in San Francisco.

By mid-August of 1967, it was quite certain that she would run for Congress in her home county of San Mateo. The office was open by virtue of the death of conservative Republican J. Arthur Younger, and a special mid-term election was called. She opposed 12 rival candidates and lost out to Pete McCloskey for a variety of reasons, some of which included the handicap of what the press termed amateur campaign management, inexperience with state party factionalism, and her late entry into the race.

Her speech in defeat was gracious and it was far from the end of her political career.

In 1968, a presidential election year, she offered her services to the Speakers Bureau of the National Republican Committee, which kept her busy from January through November. She campaigned in 21 states, 46 cities and five foreign countries, speaking as much as three times a day.

Shirley Temple's fame was a source of considerable publicity for the Republicans during the campaign. When she appeared it was big news, here and all over the world. Television stations, newspapers, and major magazines including *Time, Life* and *Look* ran features on her ad her appearances.

Her political campaigning did not detract from her devotion to MS affairs. In August of 1968, she went to Czechoslovakia as co-founder and vice-president of the International Federation of Multiple Sclerosis Societies. There she was responsible for having the Czechs join the federation. She met with, and won over, the Minister of Health. She also joined in a discussion with a group of neurologists and bio-chemists at Charles University in Prague.

In September, she again went overseas for a 10-day fund-raising and vote-getting effort among American communities living in Europe. She visited Italy, France, West Germany, Spain and England.

Back in the U.S., she continued her GOP fund-raising and vote-getting work. In a confidential moment, Shirley revealed that she was squeezed by so many people that she sometimes came home black and blue. Other fans dragged out old Shirley Temple dolls and pictures to be autographed.

President Nixon appointed Shirley as a U.S. delegate to the United Nations General Assembly in 1969. It has been traditional for the U.S. delegation always to include a well-known celebrity in order to bring publicity to the U.N. Shirley filled that requirement easily. Her name was known in many countries, and soon she became the most sought-after dinner guest at the U.N. General Assembly. She was always cheerfully greeted by delegates of other countries in the U.N. lounges between work sessions.

Shirley explained her interest in politics. "I entertained people during the first half of my life through films, and I decided to spend the rest of my life serving people. . . ."

Shirley's performance in the General Assembly was good enough to warrant her appointment to the U.S. Preparatory Committee for the U.N.-sponsored environmental conference in Stockholm in 1972. She was praised for being well-informed on various issues, and was admired for her common sense approach in conducting negotiations. The Sarah Coventry Trophy for being named Woman of the Year at the U.N. was presented to her in 1972.

But 1972 also brought Shirley bad news. She was struck with cancer of the breast which resulted in a mastectomy.

She was brave about the calamity, and offered to share her experience and feelings with the world. She wrote articles for movie and women's magazines, urging women to check regularly for lumps in their breasts. She assured them that a cure was possible, and that life was much more important than one's vanity.

Then, as never before, Shirley Temple proved that her real concern was for the average person.

Women deluged her with letters, all sympathetic and grateful. They thanked her for speaking on the quality of life when so much attention had been concentrated on trivia. Shirley's message to American women was that it is the head, heart, mind and the spirit that shapes a woman's life.

Shirley turned down requests from the American Cancer Society to become part of their volunteer force—for her heart still belonged to the task of finding a cure for MS.

In 1974, she was approved as U.S. Ambassador to Ghana in Africa.

Although Shirley Temple's first film was a spoof of *The Front Page*, and public figures, she was a headliner all through her active film-making career, and in her later career as concerned citizen and public servant.

In the course of her long career, Shirley appeared with most of radio's top comedians. Here, she is going over a script with Fred Allen.

Shirley Temple Black and her husband, Charles Black.

In 1957, at age 29, Shirley returned to show business. Above, she is being fitted for an elaborate gown by Marie Johnson, to be worn on the *Shirley Temple Storybook*, an hour-long presentation of fairy tales.

Whenever Shirley appeared in her TV series, exquisite and costly gowns were designed for her.

(Above) Charlton Heston and Claire Bloom are shown with Shirley after their appearance on the *Shirley Temple Storybook*. The two stars were her first guests. Shirley was the narrator.

(Left) In 1958, Shirley autographs a copy of her *Shirley Temple Storybook* at an autograph party in a Los Angeles bookstore.

During the 1960-61 season, NBC-TV presented 13 full-hour colorcasts in which Shirley served as hostess. She also starred in several of them. The program was called *The Shirley Temple Show*.

The Shirley Temple Show, in 1960, featured Shirley as Widow Winters. In this scene, she nurses an Indian boy (David Kent) back to health. The story was based on Louisa May Alcott's historical adventure, *Onawandah*.

(Above) The Black family is shown here in December, 1960, when Shirley was doing her *Shirley Temple Show* for NBC-TV. Her children are Susan, Lori and Charles, Jr.

(Left) Candidate Shirley Temple Black ran for Congress in California in 1967. She lost out to Pete McCloskey.

Shirley made many appearances to raise funds for multiple sclerosis. This photo was furnished to the Shirley Collectors Club, which holds an auction each year to honor Shirley's birthday and raise money.

A photograph of Mrs. Shirley Temple Black in action as a United States delegate to the United Nations. This photograph appeared in *Hola*, a Spanish magazine.

A year before the First Lady, Mrs. Gerald Ford, captured the headlines when she suddenly underwent surgery for breast cancer, diplomat Shirley Temple Black had the same experience. Here, she appears on *The Mike Douglas Show* to reassure the world that a mastectomy is not the end of a woman's life.

Shirley made an appearance on *The Mike Douglas Show* in May of 1974, during which she talked about the many projects that were close to her heart.